Geometry for Primary Grade 3

Introduction 2

Letter to Parents 4

Letter to Students 5

Student Progress Chart...6

NCTM Standards Correlation 8

UNIT 1: Basic Ideas of Geometry
Assessment 9
Line Segments...10
Line Segments...11
Line Segments...12
Line Segments...13
Angles..14
Angles..15
Angles..16
Open and Closed Curves...................................17
Open and Closed Curves...................................18
Lines and Pieces 19
Problem Solving..20
Problem Solving..21

UNIT 2: Plane Figures
Assessment 22
Identifying Plane Figures 23
Attributes of Plane Figures 24
Exploring Plane Figures 25
Exploring Plane Figures 26
Attributes of Plane Figures 27
Alike/Not Alike 28
Similar Figures 29
Problem Solving..30

UNIT 3: Solid Figures
Assessment 31
Surfaces 32
Faces, Edges, Vertices 33
Faces, Edges, Vertices 34
Faces, Edges, Vertices 35
Identifying Solids..36
Identifying Solids..37
Identifying Solids..38
Problem Solving..39

UNIT 4: Congruence and Symmetry
Assessment 40
Identifying Congruent Figures.........................41
Exploring Congruent Figures 42
Exploring Congruent Figures 43
Identifying Lines of Symmetry........................44
Identifying Lines of Symmetry........................45
Identifying Lines of Symmetry........................46
Drawing Lines of Symmetry............................47
Problem Solving..48
Problem Solving..49

UNIT 5: Perimeter, Area, and Volume
Assessment 50
Exploring Perimeter 51
Measuring Perimeter 52
Measuring Perimeter 53
Measuring Perimeter 54
Measuring Perimeter 55
Problem Solving..56
Problem Solving..57
Problem Solving..58
Finding Area 59
Finding Area 60
Finding Area 61
Finding Area 62
Problem Solving..63
Finding Volume 64
Finding Volume 65
Finding Volume 66
Finding Volume 67
Use Manipulatives to Find Volume 68

UNIT 6: Fractions Using Pictorial Models
Assessment 69
Fractional Parts of a Whole 70
Fractional Parts of a Whole 71
Fractional Parts of a Whole 72
Equivalent Fractions 73
Equivalent Fractions...74
Equivalent Fractions...75
Equivalent Fractions...76
Equivalent Fractions...77
Comparing Fractions...78
Comparing Fractions...79
Comparing Fractions...80
Comparing Fractions...81
Whole Numbers and Mixed Numbers 82
Whole Numbers and Mixed Numbers 83
Whole Numbers and Mixed Numbers 84
Problem Solving..85
Problem Solving..86

UNIT 7: Coordinate Graphs
Assessment 87
Number Pairs...88
Number Pairs...89
Drawing a Coordinate Graph 90
Using a Coordinate Graph 91
Problem Solving..92
Problem Solving..93
Problem Solving..94

ANSWER KEY...95

Geometry for Primary Grade 3

Helping students form an understanding of geometric shapes is a challenging task. In order to help students learn to recognize shapes, they must be approached in terms that will have meaning for them. The National Council of Teachers of Mathematics (NCTM) has set specific standards to help students become confident in their mathematical abilities. Geometry is an important component of the primary mathematics curriculum because geometric knowledge, relationships, and insights are useful in everyday situations and are connected to other mathematical topics and school subjects. *Geometry for Primary Grade 3* blends the vision of the NCTM Standards.

Geometry for Primary Grade 3 provides you with the opportunity to expand students' knowledge of geometry. Activities requiring the identification of sides, corners, line segments, and congruent figures are presented. Students recognize the shapes and names for solid and plane figures. They also identify the number of sides and corners of squares, rectangles, and triangles. Recognizing square corners and line segments, same size and same shape, symmetric figures, and lines of symmetry are skills included in this book. Students continue their study by finding perimeter, area, and volume, and by learning the meaning of fractions and fractional parts of a whole. Students conclude their study by working with coordinate graphs.

Art activities that involve symmetry will enhance the learning experience for most students, as will the discussion of shapes in the classroom or a scavenger hunt for shapes through the pages of magazines. Providing experiences for exploration of straight and curved lines in the classroom will make textbook pages come to life.

It is essential that students be given sufficient concrete examples of geometric concepts. Manipulatives that can be used to reinforce the skills are recommended on the activity pages.

Organization

Seven units cover the basic geometric skills presented in the third grade: basic ideas of geometry; plane figures; solid figures; congruence and symmetry; perimeter, area, and volume; fractions using pictorial models; and coordinate graphs. In *Geometry for Primary Grade 3,* the mathematics curriculum is presented so that students can:

- formulate and solve problems from everyday and mathematical situations

- describe, model, draw, and classify shapes

- investigate and predict the results of combining, subdividing, and changing shapes

- develop spatial sense

- relate geometric ideas to number and measurement ideas

- recognize and appreciate geometry in their world

- understand the attributes of length, perimeter, and area

- develop concepts of fractions and mixed numbers.

© Steck-Vaughn Company

Geometry for Primary Grade 3

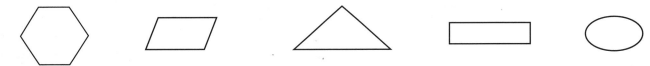

Use

The activities in this book are designed for independent use by students who have had instruction in the specific skills covered in the lessons. Copies of the activity sheets can be given to individuals or pairs of students for completion. When students are familiar with the content of the worksheets, they can be assigned as homework.

To begin, determine the implementation that fits your students' needs and your classroom structure. The following plan suggests a format for this implementation.

1. **Administer** the Assessment tests to establish baseline information on each student. These tests may also be used as post-tests when students have completed a unit.

2. **Explain** the purpose of the worksheets to the class.

3. **Review** the mechanics of how you want students to work with the activities. Do you want them to work in pairs? Are the activities for homework?

4. **Introduce** students to the process and purpose of the activities. Work with students when they have difficulty. Give them only a few pages at a time to avoid pressure.

Additional Notes

1. Parent Communication. Send the Letter to Parents home with students.

2. Student Communication. Encourage students to share the Letter to Students with their parents.

3. Manipulatives. Manipulatives are recommended at the bottom of the activity pages. This optional feature can help you provide concrete examples to reinforce geometric concepts.

4. NCTM Standards Correlation. This chart helps you with your lesson planning. An icon for each standard is included on the student page so that you can tell at a glance what skill is being reinforced on the page.

5. Student Progress Chart. Duplicate the grid sheets found on pages 6-7. Record student names in the left column. Note date of completion of each lesson for each student.

6. Have fun! Working with these activities can be fun as well as meaningful for you and your students.

Dear Parent:

During this school year, our class will be working with mathematical skills. We will be completing activity sheets that provide enrichment in the area of geometry. This includes skills in problem solving, geometry and spatial sense, fractions, patterns, and coordinate graphs.

From time to time, I may send home activity sheets. To best help your child, please consider the following suggestions:

- *Provide a quiet place to work.*
- *Go over the directions together.*
- *Encourage your child to do his or her best.*
- *Check the lesson when it is complete.*
- *Go over your child's work, and note improvements as well as problems.*

Help your child maintain a positive attitude about mathematics. Let your child know that each lesson provides an opportunity to have fun and to learn. If your child expresses anxiety about these strategies, help him or her understand what causes the stress. Then talk about ways to eliminate math anxiety.

Above all, enjoy this time you spend with your child. He or she will feel your support, and skills will improve with each activity completed.

Thank you for your help!

Cordially,

Dear Student:

This year you will be working in many areas in mathematics. The activities in this program concentrate on the area of geometry. You will work with lines, sides, and corners; plane and solid figures; matching shapes that are the same shape and size; lines of symmetry; measuring the distance around and the area of figures; equal parts of a figure; and using a graph to find spots on a map. You will get to color, draw, count, and sort shapes, measure size, write in code, and solve problems. These activities will show you fun ways to practice geometry!

As you complete the worksheets, remember the following:

- Read the directions carefully.
- Read each question carefully.
- Check your answers after you complete the activity.

You will learn many ways to solve math problems. Have fun as you develop these skills!

Sincerely,

STUDENT PROGRESS CHART

STUDENT NAME	UNIT 1 BASIC IDEAS OF GEOMETRY												UNIT 2 PLANE FIGURES								UNIT 3 SOLID FIGURES								UNIT 4 CONGRUENCE & SYMMETRY								
	10	11	12	13	14	15	16	17	18	19	20	21	23	24	25	26	27	28	29	30	32	33	34	35	36	37	38	39	41	42	43	44	45	46	47	48	49

STUDENT PROGRESS CHART

STUDENT NAME	UNIT 5 PERIMETER, AREA, AND VOLUME																		UNIT 6 FRACTIONS USING PICTORIAL MODELS																			UNIT 7 COORDINATE GRAPHS							
	51	52	53	54	55	56	57	58	59	60	61	62	63	64	65	66	67	68	70	71	72	73	74	75	76	77	78	79	80	81	82	83	84	85	86	88	89	90	91	92	93	94

© Steck-Vaughn Company

Geometry 3, SV 5807-8

NCTM STANDARDS CORRELATION

NCTM Standard	Unit 1	Unit 2	Unit 3	Unit 4	Unit 5	Unit 6	Unit 7
? **1: Problem Solving** • formulate problems from everyday and mathematical situations	20, 21	26, 27, 30	39	42, 45, 48, 49	54, 56, 57, 58, 60, 63, 66	72, 77, 80, 81, 85, 86	92, 93, 94
9: Geometry & Spatial Sense • describe shapes		23, 24, 25, 26, 27, 30	32, 33, 34, 35, 39				
9: Geometry & Spatial Sense • draw shapes		28			60, 62		
9: Geometry & Spatial Sense • classify shapes		23, 24, 25, 27, 28, 29	35, 36, 37, 38				
9: Geometry & Spatial Sense • changing shapes	17, 18, 20, 21	30, 31, 32, 33, 34, 35	41, 42, 43				
9: Geometry & Spatial Sense • combining, subdividing, and changing shapes		27, 28		41, 42, 43, 44, 45, 46, 47, 48, 49		70, 71, 72, 73, 74, 75, 76, 77, 78, 79, 80, 81, 82, 83, 84, 85, 86	
9: Geometry & Spatial Sense • develop spatial sense	10, 11, 12, 13, 14, 15, 16, 17, 18, 19, 20, 21	23, 24, 25, 26, 28, 29	32, 33, 34, 35, 39	41, 42, 43, 44, 45, 46, 47, 48, 49		85	88, 89, 90, 91, 92, 93, 94
9: Geometry & Spatial Sense • recognize and appreciate geometry in their world		25, 26, 30	36, 37, 38, 39	42, 45, 47, 48, 49	54, 55, 56, 57, 58, 60, 66	72, 75, 78, 80, 81	88, 89, 93
9: Geometry & Spatial Sense • relate geometric ideas to number and measurement ideas	19	23, 24, 25, 26, 27	32, 33, 34, 35, 39		51, 52, 53, 54, 55, 56, 57, 58, 59, 60, 61, 62, 63, 64, 65, 66, 67, 68	70, 71, 72, 73, 74, 75, 76, 77, 78, 79, 80, 81, 82, 83, 84, 86	88, 89, 90, 91, 92
10: Measurement • understand the attributes of length					51, 52, 53, 54, 55, 56, 57, 58		
10: Measurement • understand the attributes of area					59, 60, 61, 62, 63		
10: Measurement • understand the attributes of volume					64, 65, 66, 67, 68		
12: Fractions & Decimals • develop concepts of fractions and mixed numbers						70, 71, 72, 73, 74, 75, 76, 77, 78, 79, 80, 81, 82, 83, 84, 85, 86	

BASIC IDEAS OF GEOMETRY

Unit 1: Assessment

Name each line segment in two ways.

1.

_____

_____, _____

2.

_____

_____, _____

Write how many angles there are in each figure.

3.

_____

4.

_____

5. Which of the following shapes are open curves?

a.   b.   c.   d.

e.   f.   g.   h.

_____

Line Segments

A   B

D

C

Look at the picture at the right.
Which is a line, *AB* or *CD*?

Remember

A **line** is straight. It goes on forever in both directions. The arrows on a line mean that it goes on forever. A **line segment** is straight. It has 2 endpoints. A line segment is part of a line.

AB is a line (*AB*); *CD* is a line segment (*CD*).

Is this a line segment? Write *yes* or *no*.

1.   **2.**   **3.**

_____   _____   _____

Name each line segment in two ways.

4.
C   D

5.
Q   R

_____   _____

Write *line* or *line segment* for each.

6.
N   M

7.
Y   Z

8.
S   T

_____   _____   _____

Name each line in two ways.

9.
O   P

10.
D   E

_____   _____

Make lines and line segments on Graph Paper.

BASIC IDEAS OF GEOMETRY

Line Segments

Ring each figure made from line segments.

1.

2.

3.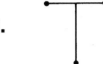

Write *line* or *line segment* for each.
Then write two names for each.

4.

_____

_____, _____

5.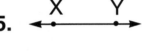

_____

_____, _____

6.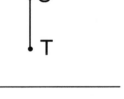

_____

_____, _____

....

Draw line segments to connect the dots below in alphabetical order.

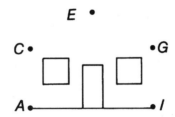

Ring the correct answer.

7. How many line segments are there?

   a. four   **b.** five   **c.** six

8. Which letters show the endpoints for the line segments of the roof?

   a. *C, E, G* **b.** *C, A, I* **c.** *A, I, G*

9. Which line segment is the longest?

   a. $\overline{CE}$ **b.** $\overline{AC}$ **c.** $\overline{AI}$

Duplicate line segments on Geoboards.

Name_____ Date _____

Line Segments

Is this a line segment? Write *yes* or *no*.

1.

_____

2.

_____

3.

_____

4.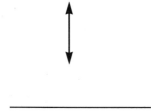

_____

5.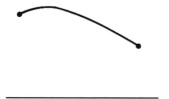

_____

6.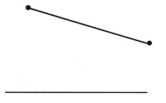

_____

. . . .

Name each line segment in two ways.

7.
J   K

_____, _____

8. •————————•
S   T

_____, _____

9. •————————•
V   W

_____, _____

10. •————————•
E   D

_____, _____

Make line segments on Graph Paper. ⬭

12

Name_____ Date _____

Line Segments

Write *line* or *line segment* for each.

1.

_____

2.
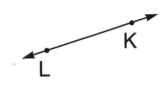

_____

3.

_____

4.
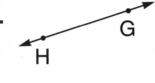

_____

5.
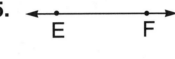

_____

6.

_____

Name each line in two ways.

7.

_____, _____

8.

_____, _____

9.

_____, _____

10.

_____, _____

11.

_____, _____

12.
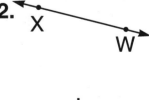

_____, _____

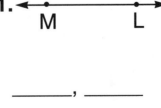
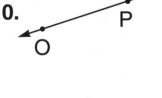

Make and label lines and line segments on Graph Paper. ▢

Angles

Look at the pictures at the right. Are
these right angles?

A

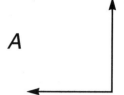

Remember

Two sides of a shape meet to form an angle.
Any angle that forms a square corner is a
right angle. It does not matter how it is
placed on the page. Take the corner of your
paper and try to fit it into Figure *A*. It should
just fit. It should also just fit into Figure *B*.

B

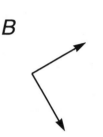

Both Figure *A* and Figure *B* are right angles.

....

Is the figure an angle? Write *yes* or *no*.

1.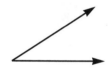

2.

3.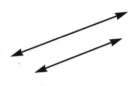

_____

_____

_____

Is the figure a right angle? Write *yes* or *no*.

4.

5.

6.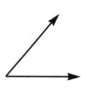

_____

_____

_____

Write how many angles there are in each figure.

7.

8.

9.

_____

_____

_____

Duplicate figures on Geoboards. ⬤

BASIC IDEAS OF GEOMETRY

Angles

Is this a right angle? Write *yes* or *no*.

1.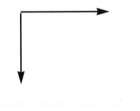

_____

2.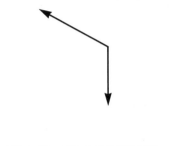

_____

3.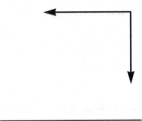

_____

4.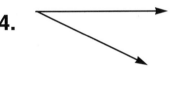

_____

5.

_____

6.

_____

Write how many angles there are in each figure.

7.

_____

8.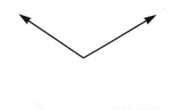

_____

9.

_____

10.

_____

11.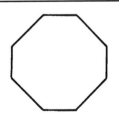

_____

12.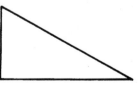

_____

Draw angles with Wooden or Plastic Triangles. ▢

© Steck-Vaughn Company

Unit 1: Basic Ideas of Geometry
Geometry 3, SV 5807-8

Name _____ Date _____

Angles

Is this a right angle? Write *yes* or *no*.

1.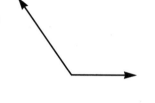

_____

2.

_____

3.

_____

4.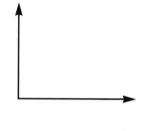

_____

5.

_____

6.

_____

· ·

Write how many angles there are in each figure.

7.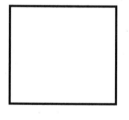

_____

8.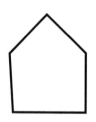

_____

9.

_____

10.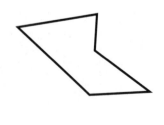

_____

11.

_____

12.

_____

Measure angles with Protractors. ⬭

© Steck-Vaughn Company

Unit 1: Basic Ideas of Geometry
Geometry 3, SV 5807-8

Open and Closed Curves

There are two kinds of curves. They are **open curves** and **closed curves**.

Look at the *closed curves* in this box. They have no beginning or end. They keep going forever. Trace them with your pencil.

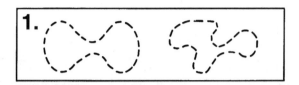

Look at the *open curves* in this box. They have a beginning and an end. Trace them with your pencil. They are **simple curves**.

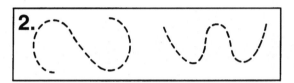

Here are two closed curves that are not simple. When you follow each curve with your pencil, you cross your path. Try it. In the box, draw one more closed curve that is not simple.

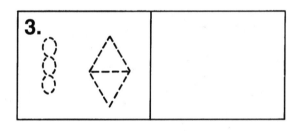

Here are two open curves that are not simple. Draw two more open curves that are not simple in the box.

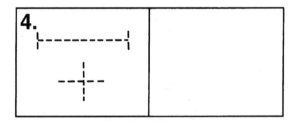

Look at the numbers in this box.
- Shade all numbers that are simple closed curves.
- Draw an X on numbers that are closed and not simple curves.
- Draw a box around all numbers that are simple open curves.
- Ring all numbers that are not closed and not simple.

5.   0   1   2   3   4   5   6   7   8   9

Make closed curves on Geoboards.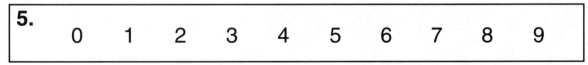

Name _____ Date _____

Open and Closed Curves

Some shapes are **open curves**, and some shapes are **closed curves**.

Here are two **closed** curves. They have no beginning or end. They keep going around and around forever. Draw two more closed curves in the box.

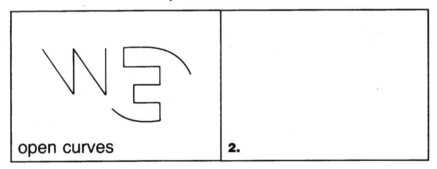

closed curves | 1.

Here are two **open** curves. They have a beginning and an end. Draw two more open curves in the box.

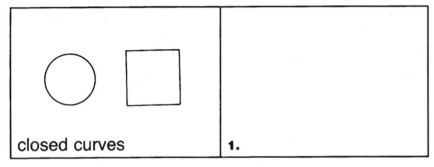

open curves | 2.

Look at the shapes in the box. Decide which are closed curves and which are open curves. Color inside the closed curves. Draw a ring around the open curves.

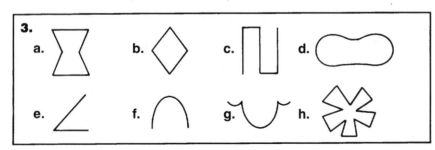

3.
a. b. c. d.
e. f. g. h.

Make closed curves on Graph Paper. ⬤

BASIC IDEAS OF GEOMETRY

Lines and Pieces

Drawing 1 straight line through a box makes 2 pieces.

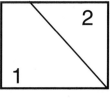

1. Draw 2 straight lines through this box. Number each new piece. How many pieces did you make?

_____

2. Can you make a different number of pieces with just 2 lines?

_____

3. Draw 3 straight lines through this box. Make the smallest number of pieces you can.

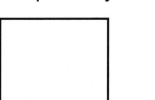

How many pieces did you make? _____

4. Make the largest number of pieces you can with 3 straight lines.

How many pieces did you make? _____

5. Make the smallest number of pieces you can with 4 straight lines.

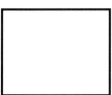

How many pieces did you make? _____

6. Make the largest number of pieces you can with 4 straight lines.

How many pieces did you make? _____

Make squares and rectangles with Tangram pieces.

BASIC IDEAS OF GEOMETRY

Problem Solving

Here are several shapes. You can draw each one with just one line.

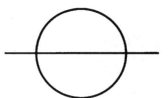

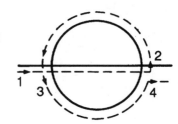

- Look at the shape carefully.
- Place your pencil where you want to start.
- Draw the shape without lifting your pencil from the paper.
- Do not draw the same line twice.
- When you have drawn the shape, add arrows to show which way you drew each line.
- Number the arrows to show the order that you drew the lines.

The shape at the right is done for you.

1.

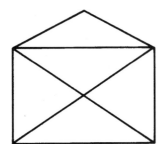

2.

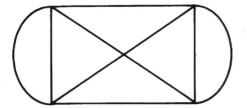

Draw shapes on Graph Paper. ❓⬜

BASIC IDEAS OF GEOMETRY

Problem Solving

The telephone poles in the drawing appear to become smaller and smaller because they are drawn in perspective. Things close to us seem larger, and things far away seem smaller.

1. Draw the telephone pole that would be the closest to you.

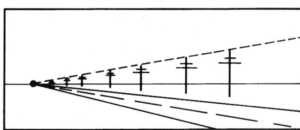

2. Look at the dot and top line. Use your ruler to draw the bottom line for the telephone poles.

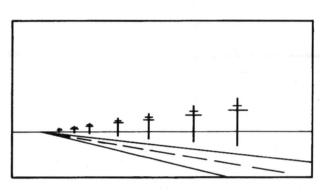

3. Draw the top line and a box that would be the one closest to you.

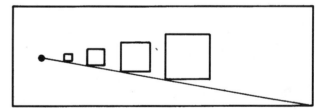

4. Draw one more tree and one more house.

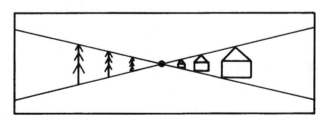

© Steck-Vaughn Company

21

Name _____   Date _____

Unit 2: Assessment

Write the name of each shape.

1.

_____

2.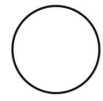

_____

3.

_____

....

Count the sides and vertices of each shape.

4.

____ sides

____ vertices

5.

____ sides

____ vertices

6.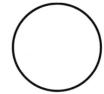

____ sides

____ vertices

....

Write the name of each figure.

7. It has no sides and no
vertices.

_____

8. It has 4 equal sides
and 4 right angles.

_____

Name _____ Date _____

Identifying Plane Figures

Remember

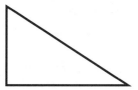 

A **triangle** has 3 sides and 3 vertices.

A **square** has 4 sides of equal length, 4 vertices, and 4 right angles.

A **rectangle** has 4 sides, 4 vertices, and 4 right angles.

A **circle** has no sides and no angles.

Write the name of each shape.

1. [rectangle]   **2.**   **3.** [triangle]

_____ _____ _____

Count the sides and vertices of each shape.

4.   **5.**   **6.**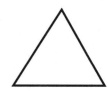

_____ sides   _____ sides   _____ sides

_____ vertices   _____ vertices   _____ vertices

7. _____ sides

_____ vertices

Sort Attribute Blocks by number of sides and vertices.

PLANE FIGURES

Attributes of Plane Figures

 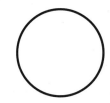 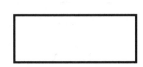 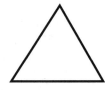

Write *triangle, square, rectangle,* or *circle* to answer the question. Each question may have more than one answer.

1. Which figure has four corners? _____

2. Which figure does not have four right angles? _____

3. Which figure is made from line segments? _____

....

Write the letter of each figure below that fits each description.

4. four equal sides _____

5. no line segments _____

6. six corners _____

7. four right angles _____

8. three sides _____

a. **b.** **c.**

d. **e.** **f.**

Match Attribute Blocks to shapes on page. ⬤

Name _____ Date _____

Exploring Plane Figures

Name the figure that each looks like.

1.

_____

2.

_____

3.

_____

4.

_____

5.

_____

6.

_____

Draw a line from the description to the name of the figure.

7. 4 sides and 4 corners
All sides are not the same length.

8. 3 sides and 3 corners

9. 4 sides and 4 corners
All sides are the same length.

10. 5 sides and 5 corners

11. 0 sides and 0 corners

circle

pentagon

rectangle

square

triangle

Name two things in the kitchen of your home that are shaped like each figure listed.

12. Square   _____   _____

13. Rectangle   _____   _____

14. Circle   _____   _____

Describe Attribute Blocks.

Name _____ Date _____

Exploring Plane Figures

Name the figure that each looks like.

1. _____	2. 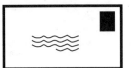 _____	3. _____
4. _____	5. _____	6. _____

Draw a line from the description to the name of the figure.

7. 4 segments and 4 angles
   All segments are the same length.

8. 4 segments and 4 angles
   All segments are not the same length.

9. 3 segments and 3 angles

10. 0 sides and 0 angles

11. 5 segments and 5 angles

circle

pentagon

rectangle

square

triangle

12. Mr. Lewis is driving to the store.
    He slows when he sees a yield
    sign. Draw a yield sign.
    What shape is the yield sign?

_____

Match Attribute Blocks to each illustration. 🔲

Name _____ Date _____

Attributes of Plane Figures

You can use *all, some,* or *none* to describe how two sets of objects are related.

> All of the squares are figures.
>
> Some of the figures are squares.
>
> None of the squares is a triangle.

Notice that a triangle is always a figure, but a figure is not always a triangle.

A triangle is never a square.

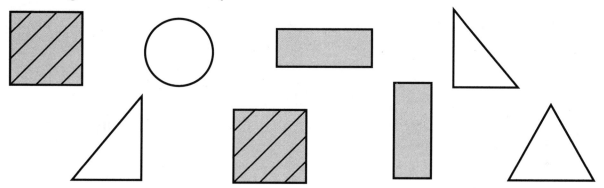

Complete. Write *All, Some,* or *None.*

1. _____ of the squares are striped.

2. _____ of the gray figures are squares.

3. _____ of the circles is striped.

4. _____ of the triangles are congruent.

5. _____ of the squares are congruent.

6. _____ of the squares are rectangles.

Sort Attribute Blocks by *all* and *some.*

PLANE FIGURES

Alike/Not Alike

Two different-size shapes that are the same in every other way
are **alike**.

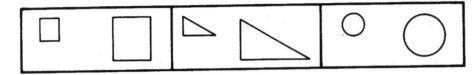

These shapes are alike.

Two different-size shapes that are different in *other* ways as well are
not alike.

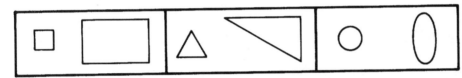

These shapes are not alike.

Ring each pair of shapes that are alike. For each pair not alike,
cross out one shape. Then draw a shape like the remaining shape.

1.

2.

3.

4.

5.

Sort Attribute Blocks by *alike* and *not alike*. ⬤

Name_____   Date _____

Similar Figures

Two different-size shapes that are the same in *every* other way are **similar figures**.

These shapes are similar. Draw a third shape that is similar.

1.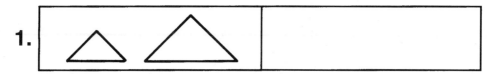

These two shapes are *not* similar. They are different in size and in *other ways*, too. Draw a third shape that is not similar.

2.

Write *yes* if the shapes are similar to each other. Write *no* if they are not.

3. ⬜ ☐ _____   **4.** ☐☐ _____   **5.** △ △ _____

6. ○ ∘ _____   **7.** ∘ ○ _____   **8.** ▯ ▯ _____

9. ⬡ ⬠ _____   **10.** ◁ ◁ _____

11. Look at these groups of shapes. Circle one group whose members are always similar.

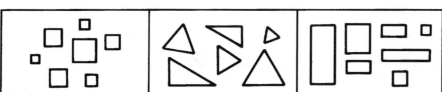

Make similar figures on Geoboards. ▢

Name _____ Date _____

Problem Solving

Name two things in your school that are shaped like each figure listed.

1. Circle   _____   _____

2. Triangle   _____   _____

3. Rectangle   _____   _____

··

Solve.

4. René closes his eyes. He puts his hand in his pocket. He feels a nickel. What shape is the nickel?

_____

5. Liza holds a CD box in her hand. What shape is the top of the box?

_____

6. Liza opens the box and takes out the CD. What shape is the top of the CD?

_____

7. Michael carried a flat object that has 4 corners. Some of the sides are the same length. All of the sides are not the same length. Michael dropped the object into a mailbox. What object did Michael carry?

_____

Name the figure that Michael's object looks like. _____

❓⬜

SOLID FIGURES

Unit 3: Assessment

Write the number of faces, edges, and vertices.

1. 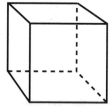   _____ faces
_____ edges
_____ vertices

2. 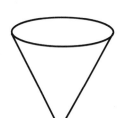   _____ faces
_____ edges
_____ vertices

Name the figure that each looks like.

3.

_____

4.

_____

5.

_____

6.

_____

© Steck-Vaughn Company   **31**

SOLID FIGURES

Surfaces

Remember

Cubes and rectangular prisms have flat surfaces.

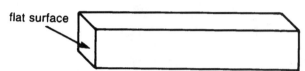

A sphere has a curved surface.   Cylinders and cones have
both flat and curved surfaces.

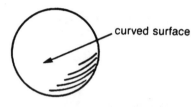

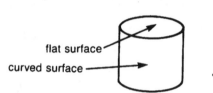

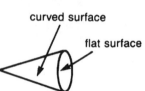

- Any flat surface of a space figure
  is called a **face**.
- An **edge** is where two faces
  meet.
- A **vertex** is where edges meet.
- This rectangular prism has 6
  faces, 12 edges, and 8 vertices.

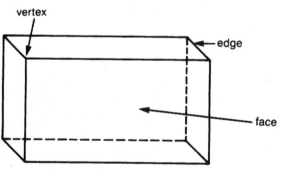

Write the number of surfaces.

1.

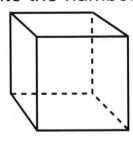

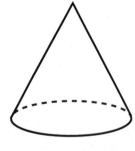

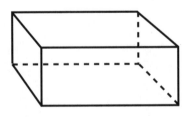

_____ flat   _____ flat   _____ flat

_____ curved   _____ curved   _____ curved

Count number of surfaces on Wooden or Plastic Geometric Solids. ⬭

Name _____ Date _____

Faces, Edges, Vertices

Write the number of surfaces.

1.  _____ flat
_____ curved

2. _____ flat
_____ curved

....

Write the number of faces, edges, and vertices.

3. _____ faces
_____ edges
_____ vertices

4. _____ faces
_____ edges
_____ vertices

5. 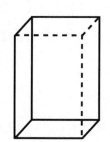 _____ faces
_____ edges
_____ vertices

6. 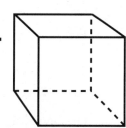 _____ faces
_____ edges
_____ vertices

7. 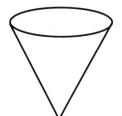 _____ faces
_____ edges
_____ vertices

8. 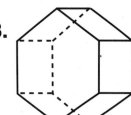 _____ faces
_____ edges
_____ vertices

Count number of surfaces on Wooden or Plastic Geometric Solids. ⬭

© Steck-Vaughn Company

33

SOLID FIGURES

Faces, Edges, Vertices

Write the number of surfaces.

1.

_____ curved

_____ flat

2.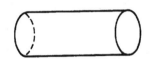

_____ curved

_____ flat

3.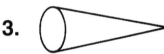

_____ curved

_____ flat

Write the number of faces, edges, and vertices.

4.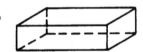

_____ faces

_____ edges

_____ vertices

5.

_____ faces

_____ edges

_____ vertices

6.

_____ faces

_____ edges

_____ vertices

Match each figure to the words that describe it.

7.

8.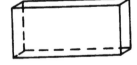

9.

a. no curved surfaces and six flat surfaces

b. one curved and two flat surfaces

c. eight flat surfaces

Check answers with Wooden or Plastic Geometric Solids.

Name_____ Date_____

SOLID FIGURES

Faces, Edges, Vertices

   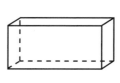

| Cube | Cone | Cylinder | Sphere | Rectangular Prism | Pyramid |

Use the solid figures to complete the table.

Figure	Faces	Edges	Vertices
Cube			
Cone			
Cylinder			
Sphere			
Rectangular Prism			
Pyramid			

Graph information from table onto Graph Paper. ⬛

© Steck-Vaughn Company

Unit 3: **Solid Figures**
Geometry 3, SV 5807-8

Name_____ Date_____

SOLID FIGURES
Identifying Solids

Look at the first figure in each row. Then ring the
object that has the same shape.

1.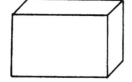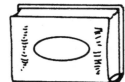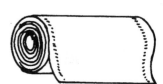

2.

3.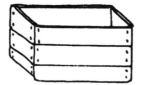

4.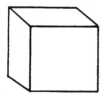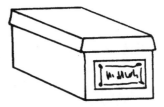

5.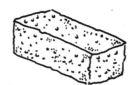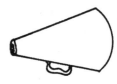

Match shapes to Wooden or Plastic Geometric Solids.

SOLID FIGURES
Identifying Solids

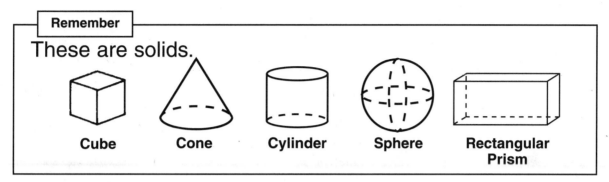

Remember

These are solids.

Cube   Cone   Cylinder   Sphere   Rectangular Prism

Name the figure that each looks like.

1.

_____

2.

_____

3.

_____

4.

_____

5.

_____

6.

_____

7.

_____

8.

_____

Make solids from clay or Modeling Dough.

SOLID FIGURES

Identifying Solids

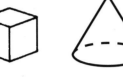   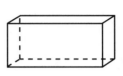

| Cube | Cone | Cylinder | Sphere | Rectangular Prism | Pyramid |

Name the figure that each looks like.

1.

_____

2.

_____

3.

_____

4.

_____

5.

_____

6.

_____

7.

_____

8.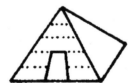

_____

9.

_____

10. Look around the room. Find 2 objects shaped like a cube. Write their names on the lines below.

_____

_____

Match shapes to Wooden or Plastic Geometric Solids. ▢

38

SOLID FIGURES

Problem Solving

     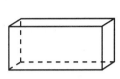

| Cube | Cone | Cylinder | Sphere | Rectangular Prism | Pyramid |

Solve the riddles. Use the solid figures.

1. I have 5 faces. All but 1 are triangles.
What am I?

_____

2. I have 6 faces. Only 2 are squares.
What am I?

_____

3. What shape is a box of tissues?

_____

4. What shape is a soup can?

_____

5. What shape is a grapefruit?

_____

Check answers with Wooden or Plastic Geometric Solids.

© Steck-Vaughn Company

      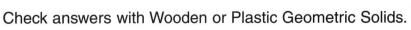

Name _____ Date _____

Unit 4: Assessment

Are the figures congruent? Write *yes* or *no*.

1.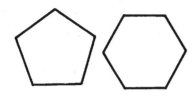

_____

2.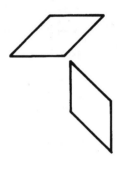

_____

Ring the figure that is congruent to the shaded figure.

3.

Is the dotted line a line of symmetry? Write *yes* or *no*.

4.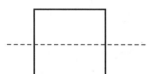

_____

5.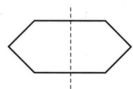

_____

6.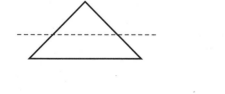

_____

© Steck-Vaughn Company

CONGRUENCE AND SYMMETRY

Identifying Congruent Figures

Jose and Sue each drew a picture of
a triangle. Are these figures congruent?

Jose's triangle   Sue's triangle

Remember

Congruent figures are the same shape and the same size.
These triangles are *not* the same size. So, they are not
congruent.

Are the figures congruent? Write *yes* or *no*.

1.

_____

2.

_____

3.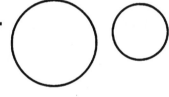

_____

4.

_____

5.

_____

6.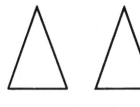

_____

7.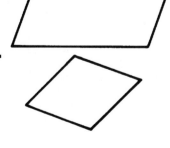

_____

8.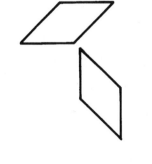

_____

9.

_____

Find congruent shapes using pattern Blocks.

CONGRUENCE AND SYMMETRY

Exploring Congruent Figures

Are the figures congruent? Write *yes* or *no*.

1.

_____

2.

_____

3.

_____

4.

_____

· ·

Ring the figure that is congruent to the shaded figure.

5.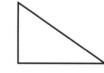

6.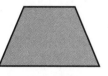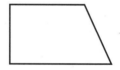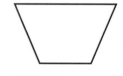

7.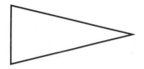

· ·

8. Leisha and Meisha are making a quilt together.
Leisha cuts a piece of fabric like the shape below. Meisha cuts a
shape that is congruent to the one Leisha cuts. Draw the shape
that Meisha cuts.

Make congruent shapes on Geoboards. ❓ ⬜

Name_____ Date _____

Exploring Congruent Figures

Ring the figure that is congruent to the shaded figure.

1.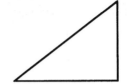

2.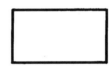

3.

4.

5.

6.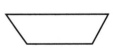

Make congruent shapes on Geoboards.

Name_____ Date _____

Identifying Lines of Symmetry

A **line of symmetry** divides a figure into two equal parts.
Each part is exactly the same size and shape.

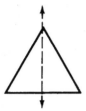

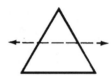

This line is a line of symmetry.   This line is not a line of symmetry.

Is the line a line of symmetry? Write *yes* or *no*.

1.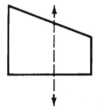

2.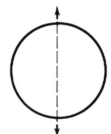

3.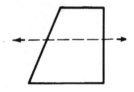

_____   _____   _____

Does each figure have a line of symmetry? Write *yes* or *no*. If *yes*,
draw the line of symmetry.

4.

5.

6.

_____   _____   _____

Trace shape and fold paper to find line of symmetry. ⬭

44

Identifying Lines of Symmetry

Trace the figure. Cut out your drawing and fold it in half.
Write *yes* or *no* to tell whether the figure has a line of symmetry.

1.   **2.**

_____ _____

3.   **4.**

_____ _____

Is the dotted line a line of symmetry? Write *yes* or *no*.

5.  **6.** 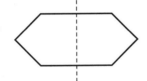 **7.**

_____ _____ _____

8. 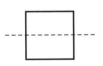 **9.**   **10.**

_____ _____ _____

....

11. In art, Mr. Ingles gave his students paper
cut in the shape to the right. He asked
his students to fold the paper along a line
of symmetry. Draw a line to show how
the students can fold the paper.

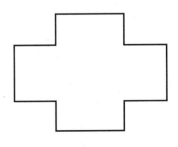

Trace shape and fold paper to find line of symmetry. ❓⬜

CONGRUENCE AND SYMMETRY

Identifying Lines of Symmetry

Does this figure have a line of symmetry?

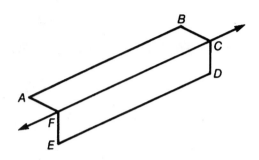

Remember

A figure has a **line of symmetry** if both parts of the figure are exactly the same size and shape. The line of symmetry does not have to go up and down or sideways. The line can go in any direction.

This figure has one line of symmetry. It is $\overleftrightarrow{CF}$.

....

Does the figure have a line of symmetry?
Write *yes* or *no*.

1.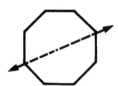

2.

3.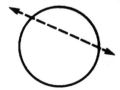

_____   _____   _____

Is the line a line of symmetry? Write *yes* or *no*.

4.

5.

6.

_____   _____   _____

Trace shape and fold paper to find line of symmetry. ⬤

Drawing Lines of Symmetry

Ring each picture in which the dotted line is a line of symmetry.

1.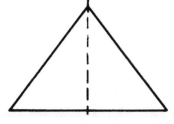

2.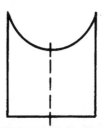

3.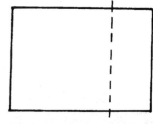

4.

5.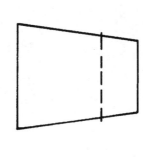

6.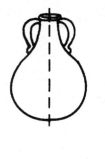

Ring each symmetric figure. Then use a ruler to draw a line of symmetry.

7.

8.

9.

10. Write three capital letters of the alphabet that are not symmetric.

_____   _____   _____

Trace shape and fold paper to find line of symmetry.

CONGRUENCE AND SYMMETRY

Problem Solving

Look at the shapes.

1. Draw boxes around the three groups of shapes that show symmetry.

2. Draw a line of symmetry through the boxes.

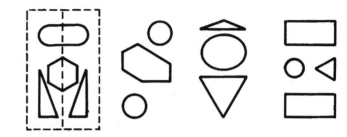

Pretend you have a camera. Your job is to take a picture showing symmetry. Look at the table. Choose a part that shows symmetry.

3. Draw a box around the part of the picture that shows symmetry.

4. Draw a line of symmetry through the box.

....

Draw a box and a line of symmetry in each picture.

5.

6.

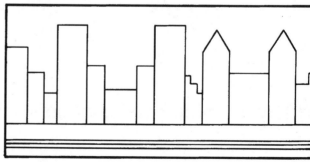

© Steck-Vaughn Company   **48**

Name_____ Date _____

Problem Solving

You can draw a line through some shapes and cut them into mirrored, or matching, parts. Look at these examples. Draw two more shapes that can be cut this way.

1.

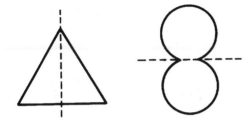

....

2. You can also cut up some letters this way. In fact, you can draw two lines through some letters, to split them into four matching parts. Draw one line or two lines to cut each letter into matching parts. Not all letters can be cut into matching parts, though!

Name_____   Date_____

Unit 5: Assessment

Use your metric ruler to measure each side. Then write the perimeter.

1.  _____

2.  _____

3. 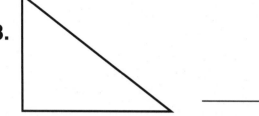 _____

....

Count to find the area in square centimeters.

4.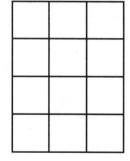

5.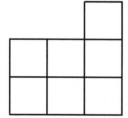

6.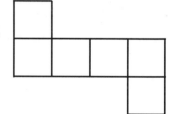

_____   _____   _____

....

Find the volume in cubic units.

7.

8.

9.

_____   _____   _____

© Steck-Vaughn Company   **Unit 5: Perimeter, Area, and Volume**
Geometry 3, SV 5807-8

PERIMETER, AREA, AND VOLUME

Exploring Perimeter

Choose a book from your desk, classroom, or home.
Find its perimeter three times. Each time use a different unit of measure. Use the units of measure in the list below.

a. width of your finger

b. width of a pencil

c. width of a paper clip

Complete the table.

	Unit of Measure	Guess	Perimeter
1.	Finger width		
2.	Pencil width		
3.	Clip width		

....

Use the width of a crayon. Find the perimeter of each figure.

4. 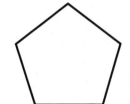   ____ units

5.    ____ units

6.    ____ units

7.    ____ units

Make a figure on Geoboard and find perimeter with a paper clip. ⬤ ⬜

Name_____ Date _____

Measuring Perimeter

What is the perimeter of the triangle at the right?

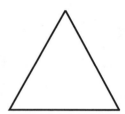

> **Remember**
>
> The **perimeter** is the distance around the
> outside of something. Use a metric ruler to
> measure each side of the shape. Each side
> of the triangle is 3 cm long.
>
> **3 + 3 + 3 = 9**

The perimeter of the triangle is 9 cm.

Use your metric ruler to measure each side. Then write the

perimeter.

1.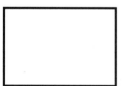

_____

2.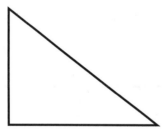

_____

3.

_____

4.

_____

5.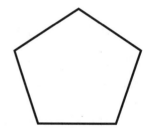

_____

6.

_____

7.

_____

8.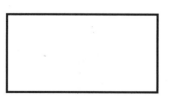

_____

9.

_____

Measure sides with a metric ruler. ⬤ ▢

© Steck-Vaughn Company
52
Unit 5: Perimeter, Area, and Volume
Geometry 3, SV 5807-8

PERIMETER, AREA, AND VOLUME

Measuring Perimeter

Perimeter is the distance around a figure.

To find the perimeter of this figure, measure each side. Then add the measures.

3 + 5 + 3 + 5 = 16

The perimeter is 16 cm.

....

Use your metric ruler to measure each side. Then find the perimeter.

1. 2 cm / 2 cm / 2 cm

_____

2. 1 cm / 3 cm / 3 cm / 1 cm
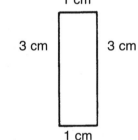

_____

3. 1 cm / 1 cm / 2 cm / 2 cm / 1 cm / 3 cm
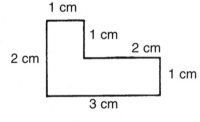

_____

4. 4 cm / 4 cm
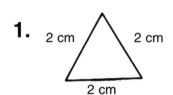

_____

5. 2 cm / 1 cm / 2 cm
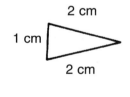

_____

6. 3 cm / 2 cm / 2 cm / 4 cm
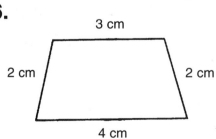

_____

Measure sides with a metric ruler. ⬤ ⬜

PERIMETER, AREA, AND VOLUME

Measuring Perimeter

Use your customary ruler to measure each side.
Then find the perimeter.

1.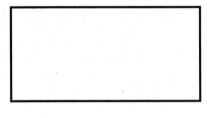

_____

2.

_____

3.

_____

4.

_____

....

5. Katy's gym class uses a mat for the broad jump. The sides of mat are 12 ft, 4 ft, 12 ft, and 4 ft. What is the perimeter of the mat?

_____

6. Sam wants to put a frame around a sign for field day. The sides of the sign are 24 in., 24 in., 18 in., and 18 in. How much wood does he need to frame the sign?

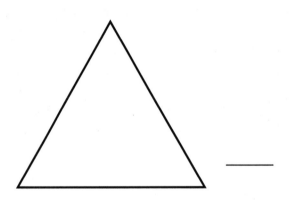

_____

Measure sides with a customary ruler.

Name _____   Date _____

Measuring Perimeter

What is the perimeter of the square?

> **Remember**
>
> Measure each side of a figure to find its perimeter. Then add the lengths of all the sides.
>
> **2 in. + 2 in. + 2 in. + 2 in. = 8 in.**

The perimeter of the square is 8 in.

Use your customary ruler to measure each side. Then write the perimeter.

1.

_____

2.

_____

....

Solve.

3. What is the perimeter of the swimming pool?

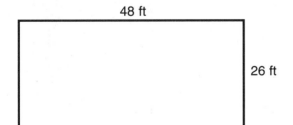

48 ft

26 ft

_____

4. What is the perimeter of this shape?

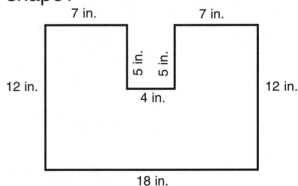

7 in.   7 in.

12 in.   5 in.   5 in.   12 in.

4 in.

18 in.

_____

Measure sides with a customary ruler. ⬤ ⬤

Name _____ Date _____

Problem Solving

Use your customary ruler to measure each side.
Then find the perimeter.

1.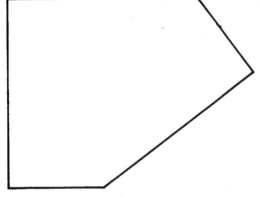

_____

2.

_____

....

Here is Pete Perimeter in his
backyard. Help him find
the perimeter of these things.

3. backyard _____

4. swimming pool _____

5. float _____

6. beach towel _____

7. newspaper _____

8. picnic table _____

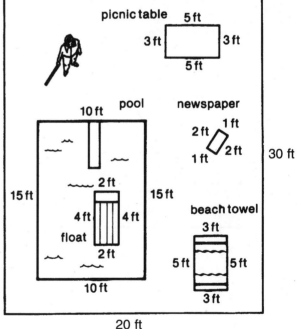

Check answers with calculator.

PERIMETER, AREA, AND VOLUME

Problem Solving

For the school play, you must build a fence along the back wall of the stage. Look at the floor plan. It shows the total perimeter and the length of all sides except the back. Add and subtract to find the length of the back wall.

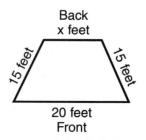

Back
x feet
15 feet
15 feet
20 feet
Front

Perimeter: 60 feet

1. Add the three lengths you do know.

___ + ___ + ___ = ___

2. Subtract this sum from the perimeter.

___ - ___ = ___

3. The length of the back side of the stage is _____ feet.

....

Find the length of side x in each shape.

4.

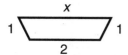

x
1   1
2

Perimeter: 7 feet
Length of side x: _____

5.

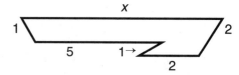

x
1   2
5   1→
2

Perimeter: 19 feet
Length of side x: _____

6.

7
1   2
x

Perimeter: 16 feet
Length of side x: _____

7.

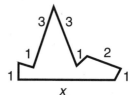

3   3
1   1   2
1   1
x

Perimeter: 17 feet
Length of side x: _____

Check answers with calculator.

PERIMETER, AREA, AND VOLUME

Problem Solving

Cut out the paper clip ruler. Choose
3 books from your desk, classroom,
or home. Find the perimeter of each
book using the paper clip ruler.
Then complete the table.

	Book	Guess	Perimeter
1.	Book 1		
2.	Book 2		
3.	Book 3		

Write the number sentence and solve.

4. The class wants to play Four Square.
Rosa will make the lines of the game.
She counts off 16 large steps for one
side. She counts the same amount of
steps for the other three sides of the
square. What is the perimeter in
steps Rosa counts?

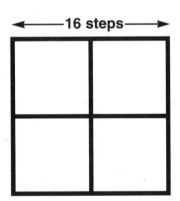

_____

Graph information from table onto Graph Paper. ❓⬜🖍

Name _____ Date _____

PERIMETER, AREA, AND VOLUME

Finding Area

The **area** of a figure is the number of square units that cover its surface.

You can count square units to find the area of a figure.

This is a square centimeter. Each side is 1 cm long.

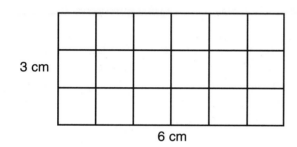

3 cm

6 cm

....

Count to find the area in square centimeters.

1.

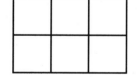

_____

2.

_____

3.

_____

4.

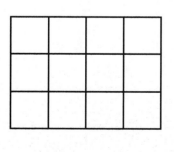

_____

5.

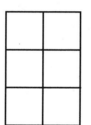

_____

6.

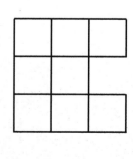

_____

Make other problems on Centimeter Graph Paper.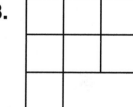

Name_____ Date_____

Finding Area

Find the area of each figure. Label your answer in square units.

1.

_____

2.

_____

3.

_____

4.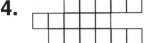

_____

5.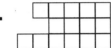

_____

6.

_____

....

Fill in squares with your pencil. Make three shapes, each with an area of 6 square units.

7.

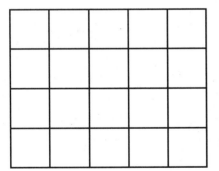

8.

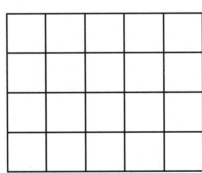

9.

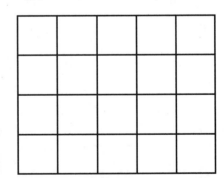

Solve.

10. Mrs. Frazer bought a rectangle-shaped rug for her classroom. One side is 3 square units wide. Another side is 4 square units long. Fill in the squares to show how many square units the rug is.

Find area of figures on Geoboard. ❓⬜🌐

60

Finding Area

Which of the two figures
has the larger area?

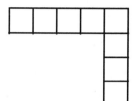

Remember

The area of a figure is the number
of square units that cover its surface.
You can count square units to find the
area of a figure. The area of the L-shaped
figure is 8 square units. The area of the
square is 9 square units.

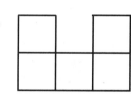

The square has the larger area.

Count to find the area in square centimeters.

1.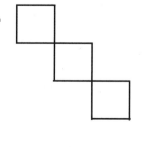

_____

2.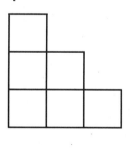

_____

3.

_____

4.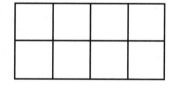

_____

5.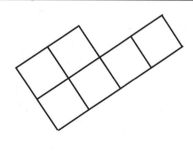

_____

6.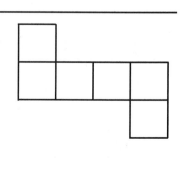

_____

Make other problems on Centimeter Graph Paper.

PERIMETER, AREA, AND VOLUME

Finding Area

Fill in squares with your pencil. Make three shapes,
each with an area of 8 square units.

1. 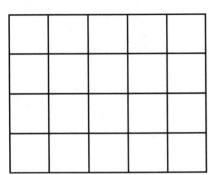 **2.** 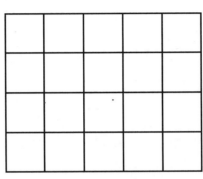 **3.**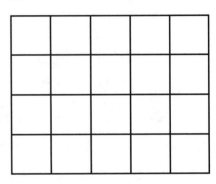

Find the area of each figure. Label your answer in square units.

4. 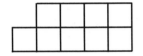   **5.** 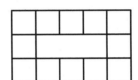   **6.**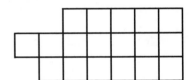

_____   _____   _____

The area of this figure is 4 square units.
Write the area of each figure below.

7. 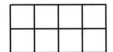   **8.** 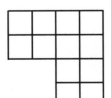   **9.**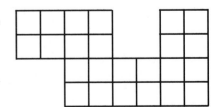

_____   _____   _____

Copy shapes with 1-inch Counting Cubes.

PERIMETER, AREA, AND VOLUME

Problem Solving

The area of each figure is made up of square units.

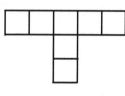
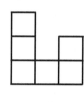
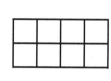

A   **B**   **C**   **D**

Complete.

1. How many square units are in Figure A? _____

2. How many square units are in Figure B? _____

3. How many square units are in Figure C? _____

4. How many square units are in Figure D? _____

5. Which figure has the greatest area? the smallest area? _____

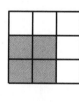
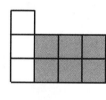
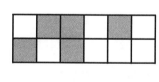

E   **F**   **G**

Complete.

6. Which figure has the most square units shaded in? _____

7. In Figure E, how many more square units need to be shaded to cover the entire area? _____

Make other problems on Centimeter Graph Paper. ❓⬜🌐

© Steck-Vaughn Company   **63**

PERIMETER, AREA, AND VOLUME

Finding Volume

What is the volume of the rectangular prism?

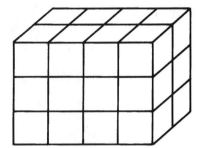

Remember

Think of making three horizontal slices.
The figure would look like this.

- Look at the front to see the number of slices.

- Each slice has 8 small cubes.

- There are 3 slices.

- There are 3 x 8, or 24 cubes.

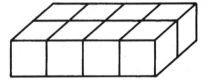

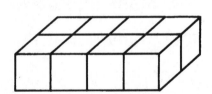

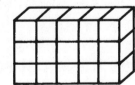

The volume of the rectangular prism is 24 cubic centimeters.

....

Count the cubes. Remember to count the cubes you cannot see.
Write the volume in cubic centimeters.

1.   _____

2. 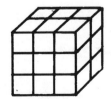 _____

3. 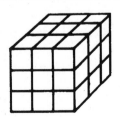 _____

4. _____

Check answers with Non-Interlocking Centimeter Cubes.

© Steck-Vaughn Company

64

Unit 5: Perimeter, Area, and Volume
Geometry 3, SV 5807-8

PERIMETER, AREA, AND VOLUME

Finding Volume

The volume of a box is equal to the number of cubic units that will fit inside it.

 = 1 cubic unit. Write the volume of each box in cubic units.

1.

_____

2.

_____

3.

_____

4.

_____

5.

_____

6.

_____

7.

_____

8.

_____

9.

_____

Check answers with Non-Interlocking Centimeter Cubes.

© Steck-Vaughn Company

Unit 5: Perimeter, Area, and Volume
Geometry 3, SV 5807-8

Finding Volume

Find the volume in cubic units.

1.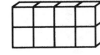

_____

2.

_____

3.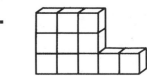

_____

4.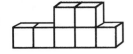

_____

5.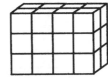

_____

6.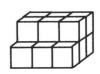

_____

7.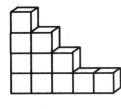

_____

8.

_____

9.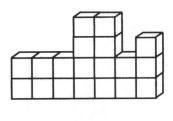

_____

Write the number sentence and solve.

10. Tran bought a new aquarium. It was 2 times bigger than his old tank. He knew the old tank had a volume of the cubes to the right. How many cubes would he need to show the volume of his new tank?

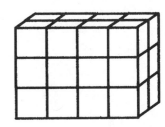

_____

Make models of figures using Counting Cubes. ❓▢⊜

Name _____ Date _____

Finding Volume

Find the volume in cubic centimeters.

1.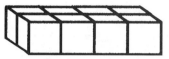

_____

2.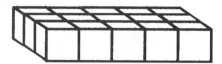

_____

3.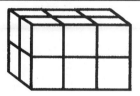

_____

4.

_____

5.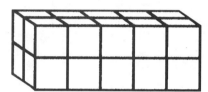

_____

6.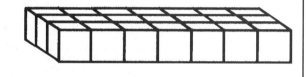

_____

 You can multiply to find the volume of a cube or a rectangular prism.

Volume = length x width x height
V = 2   x   1   x   3
V = 6 cubic centimeters

Multiply mentally to find the volume.

7.

_____

8.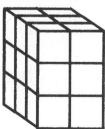

_____

9.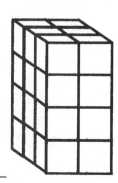

_____

Check answers with calculator.

67

PERIMETER, AREA, AND VOLUME

Use Manipulatives to Find Volume

Use cubes to build the shapes. Find the volume of each shape.

1.

_____

2.

_____

3.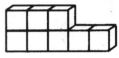

_____

4.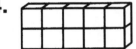

_____

5.

_____

6.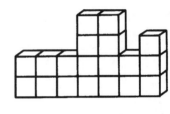

_____

7.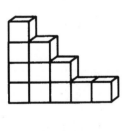

_____

8.

_____

9.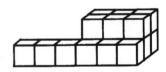

_____

Make models of figures with Non-Interlocking Centimeter Cubes. ▢ ◖

Name _____ Date _____

FRACTIONS USING PICTORIAL MODELS

Unit 6: Assessment

Write the fraction that names the shaded part.

1.

2.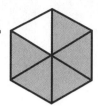

3.

_____ _____ _____

Write the equivalent fractions.

4.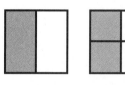

5.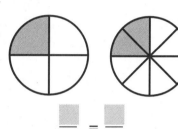

6.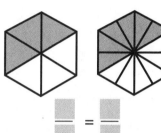

Write >, <, or = in each .

7.

$\frac{1}{2}$ $\frac{3}{4}$

8.

$\frac{2}{3}$ $\frac{3}{6}$

9.

$\frac{1}{4}$ $\frac{3}{8}$

Write the whole or the mixed number to show how much is shaded.

10.

11.

12.

_____ _____ _____

FRACTIONS USING PICTORIAL MODELS

Fractional Parts of a Whole

Scott is painting the fence in his backyard. The fence has 3 sections. Scott has painted 2 of the sections. What part of the fence did he paint?

Remember

$\frac{2}{3}$ The numerator tells how many sections were painted.
    The denominator tells how many sections there were in all.

painted section

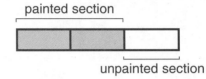

unpainted section

Scott painted $\frac{2}{3}$ of the fence.

Find the fraction that names the shaded part. Ring the letter of the correct answer.

1.

a. $\frac{1}{2}$ b. $\frac{1}{4}$
c. $\frac{3}{4}$ d. $\frac{1}{3}$

2.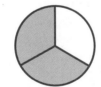

a. $\frac{2}{3}$ b. $\frac{1}{2}$
c. $\frac{1}{3}$ d. $\frac{1}{4}$

3.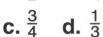

a. 1 b. $\frac{1}{3}$
c. $\frac{1}{4}$ d. $\frac{1}{2}$

Write the fraction that names the shaded part.

4. 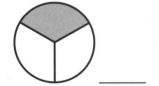 ____

5. 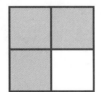 ____

6. 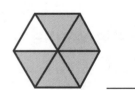 ____

7.  ____

8. 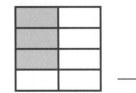 ____

9. 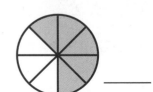 ____

Duplicate fractions using Fraction Tiles. ⬛❯

FRACTIONS USING PICTORIAL MODELS

Fractional Parts of a Whole

Draw a line.
Match the fraction with the picture that shows the correct number of shaded parts.

1.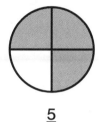

$\frac{5}{8}$

2.

$\frac{1}{2}$

3.

$\frac{3}{4}$

4.

$\frac{1}{4}$

Write the fraction that names the shaded part.

5. 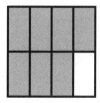 _____

6. _____

7.  _____

8. 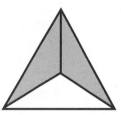 _____

9. 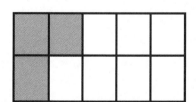 _____

10. 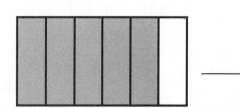 _____

Duplicate fractions using Fraction Builder Strips.

© Steck-Vaughn Company

71

Fractional Parts of a Whole

Write the fraction for the part that is shaded.

1. ☐ shaded parts   **2.** ☐ shaded parts

☐ parts in all   ☐ parts in all

3. ☐/☐   **4.** ☐/☐   **5.** 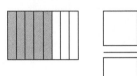 ☐/☐

Write the fraction for the part that is shaded.

6. ☐/☐   **7.** 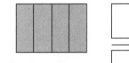 ☐/☐   **8.** ☐/☐

Write the fraction for each word name.

9. one third ☐/☐   **10.** two fifths ☐/☐   **11.** four sixths ☐/☐

Solve.

12. Sun-Yu shares $\frac{1}{4}$ of her sandwich with a friend. Shade the part of the sandwich Sun-Yu shares.

Draw and shade fractions on Graph Paper.

FRACTIONS USING PICTORIAL MODELS

Equivalent Fractions

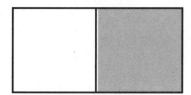 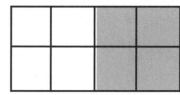

$$\frac{1}{2} = \frac{4}{8}$$

$\frac{1}{2}$ names the same amount as $\frac{4}{8}$.

$\frac{1}{2}$ and $\frac{4}{8}$ are **equivalent fractions**.

....

Ring the letter of the correct answer. Name the equivalent fractions.

1.

$\frac{2}{4} = $

2.

 =

a. $\frac{1}{2}$	**b.** 1
c. $\frac{2}{1}$	**d.** 2

a. $\frac{1}{4} = \frac{2}{8}$	**b.** $\frac{2}{8} = \frac{1}{4}$
c. $\frac{2}{6} = \frac{1}{3}$	**d.** $\frac{6}{8} = \frac{2}{4}$

....

Name the equivalent fraction.

3.

$$\frac{1}{2} = \frac{}{8}$$

4.

$$\frac{1}{2} = \frac{3}{}$$

5.

$$\frac{1}{5} = \frac{}{10}$$

Show equivalent fractions on Overhead Fraction Circles. ◖▶

FRACTIONS USING PICTORIAL MODELS

Equivalent Fractions

Name the equivalent fraction.

1.

$\frac{3}{5} = \frac{\ }{\ }$

2.

$\frac{1}{2} = \frac{\ }{\ }$

3.

$\frac{2}{5} = \frac{\ }{\ }$

Write two equivalent fractions.

4.

$\frac{\ }{\ } = \frac{\ }{\ }$

5.

$\frac{\ }{\ } = \frac{\ }{\ }$

6.

$\frac{\ }{\ } = \frac{\ }{\ }$

7.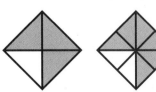

$\frac{\ }{\ } = \frac{\ }{\ }$

8.

$\frac{\ }{\ } = \frac{\ }{\ }$

9.

$\frac{\ }{\ } = \frac{\ }{\ }$

Duplicate fractions using Fraction Tiles. ◖▶

Name_____ Date _____

Equivalent Fractions

Alicia was cutting paper plates into pieces for decorations. She noticed that $\frac{1}{4}$ of a plate looked the same as $\frac{2}{8}$ of a plate. Is $\frac{1}{4}$ the same as $\frac{2}{8}$?

Remember

In this problem, $\frac{1}{4}$ and $\frac{2}{8}$ name the same amount of an area or part of a whole number. Use a model to help you see the parts.

$\frac{1}{4} = \frac{2}{8}$  $\frac{1}{4}$ $\frac{2}{8}$

$\frac{1}{4}$ is equal to $\frac{2}{8}$.

It is true that $\frac{1}{4}$ and $\frac{2}{8}$ are equivalent fractions.

....

Complete the equivalent fraction. Use the drawings to help you.

1.

$$\frac{1}{3} = \frac{}{6}$$

2.

$$\frac{1}{2} = \frac{}{8}$$

3.

$$\frac{}{} = \frac{2}{6}$$

4.

$$\frac{1}{2} = \frac{2}{}$$

5.

$$\frac{4}{5} = \frac{}{10}$$

6.

$$\frac{1}{3} = \frac{}{9}$$

Check answers using Fraction Tiles. ◖▶

© Steck-Vaughn Company

Name_____ Date _____

Equivalent Fractions

Draw a line to match the equivalent fractions.

1. $\frac{2}{5}$ **a.**   4. $\frac{2}{6}$ **a.**

2. $\frac{2}{3}$ **b.**   5. $\frac{4}{10}$ **b.**

3. $\frac{1}{3}$ **c.**   6. $\frac{4}{6}$ **c.**

···

Ring the two equivalent fractions in each row.

7. $\frac{4}{8}$ $\frac{3}{4}$ $\frac{1}{2}$

8. $\frac{2}{4}$ $\frac{1}{4}$ $\frac{2}{8}$

9. $\frac{4}{5}$ $\frac{8}{10}$ $\frac{4}{10}$

···

Shade both figures to make equivalent fractions.

10. $\frac{2}{6}$ $\frac{1}{3}$

11. $\frac{3}{4}$ $\frac{6}{8}$

12. $\frac{1}{3}$ $\frac{3}{9}$

Check answers using Fraction Tiles.

Name_____ Date_____

Equivalent Fractions

Write *true* or *false*.

1.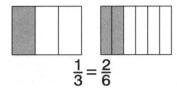

$$\frac{1}{3} = \frac{2}{6}$$

_____

2.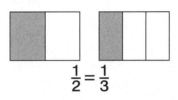

$$\frac{1}{2} = \frac{1}{3}$$

_____

3.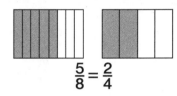

$$\frac{1}{2} = \frac{2}{4}$$

_____

4.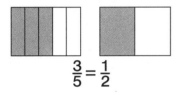

$$\frac{3}{5} = \frac{1}{2}$$

_____

5.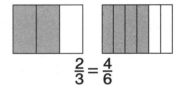

$$\frac{2}{3} = \frac{4}{6}$$

_____

6.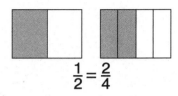

$$\frac{5}{8} = \frac{2}{4}$$

_____

....

Name the equivalent fraction.

7.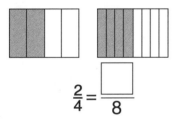

$$\frac{2}{4} = \frac{\square}{8}$$

8.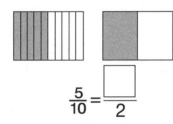

$$\frac{5}{10} = \frac{\square}{2}$$

9.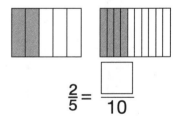

$$\frac{2}{5} = \frac{\square}{10}$$

10.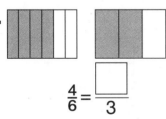

$$\frac{4}{6} = \frac{\square}{3}$$

11.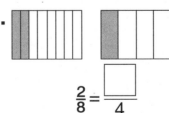

$$\frac{2}{8} = \frac{\square}{4}$$

12.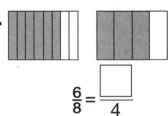

$$\frac{6}{8} = \frac{\square}{4}$$

13. Elaine and Joe each bought small pizzas for lunch. Elaine ate $\frac{1}{2}$ of her pizza. Joe ate the same amount of his pizza. Shade the amount of pizza Joe ate. Name the equivalent fraction.

$$\frac{1}{2} = \frac{\square}{4}$$

Duplicate fractions using Fraction Builder Strips. ❓◻◗

FRACTIONS USING PICTORIAL MODELS

Comparing Fractions

Ellen's mother baked two loaves of bread. She cut each loaf into 8 pieces. $\frac{6}{8}$ of the whole-wheat loaf is left. $\frac{5}{8}$ of the oatmeal loaf is left. Which loaf has more pieces left?

Remember

You can compare fractions to find the loaf that has more pieces left.

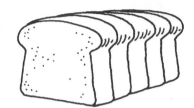

whole-wheat loaf   oatmeal loaf
The denominators are   Compare the
the same.   numerators.

$\frac{⑥}{8}$ ⟵——— same ———⟶ $\frac{⑤}{8}$
is greater than

There are more pieces of the whole-wheat loaf left.

You can use a drawing to help you compare fractions.

Write >, <, or = in each ◯ .

1.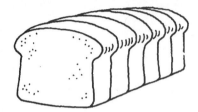

$\frac{1}{3}$ ◯ $\frac{2}{3}$

2.

$\frac{1}{2}$ ◯ $\frac{3}{4}$

3.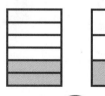

$\frac{2}{6}$ ◯ $\frac{1}{3}$

4.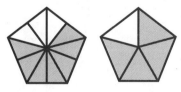

$\frac{7}{10}$ ◯ $\frac{4}{5}$

5.

$\frac{5}{6}$ ◯ $\frac{1}{3}$

6.

$\frac{1}{8}$ ◯ $\frac{1}{4}$

Lay Fraction Tiles on top of each other to check answers.

Comparing Fractions

Draw a line under the fraction that is more.

1. $\frac{1}{3}$ $\frac{2}{3}$

2. $\frac{1}{2}$ $\frac{3}{4}$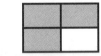

3. $\frac{3}{7}$  $\frac{1}{7}$

4. $\frac{5}{8}$ $\frac{1}{4}$

Compare. Write >, <, or = in each ◯ .

5.
$\frac{1}{6}$ ◯ $\frac{4}{6}$

6.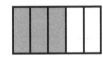
$\frac{3}{5}$ ◯ $\frac{4}{10}$

7.
$\frac{2}{3}$ ◯ $\frac{1}{3}$

8.
$\frac{1}{4}$ ◯ $\frac{2}{6}$

9.
$\frac{6}{8}$ ◯ $\frac{3}{4}$

10.
$\frac{5}{9}$ ◯ $\frac{8}{9}$

Lay Fraction Tiles on top of each other to check answers.

Comparing Fractions

Compare. Write <, >, or = in each ◯ .

1.

$\frac{1}{3}$ ◯ $\frac{2}{3}$

2.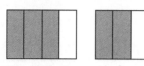

$\frac{3}{4}$ ◯ $\frac{2}{4}$

3.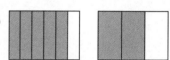

$\frac{5}{6}$ ◯ $\frac{2}{3}$

4.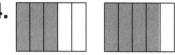

$\frac{3}{5}$ ◯ $\frac{4}{5}$

5.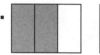

$\frac{2}{3}$ ◯ $\frac{4}{6}$

6.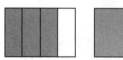

$\frac{3}{4}$ ◯ $\frac{1}{2}$

7.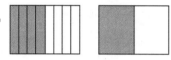

$\frac{4}{8}$ ◯ $\frac{1}{2}$

8.

$\frac{3}{5}$ ◯ $\frac{3}{8}$

9.

$\frac{2}{5}$ ◯ $\frac{4}{5}$

....

10. A bowl of muffin batter contains $\frac{1}{3}$ cup of oil and $\frac{2}{3}$ cup of milk. Do the muffins have more milk or more oil?

_____

Check answers with Fraction Builder Strips. ❓ ⬜ ❯

FRACTIONS USING PICTORIAL MODELS

Comparing Fractions

Compare. Circle the letter of the correct answer.

1.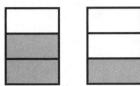

  a. $\frac{2}{1} > \frac{1}{2}$ **b.** $\frac{2}{3} > \frac{1}{3}$

  c. $\frac{2}{3} < \frac{1}{3}$ **d.** $\frac{1}{2} < \frac{2}{3}$

2.

  a. $\frac{3}{8} > \frac{1}{4}$ **b.** $\frac{5}{8} > \frac{3}{4}$

  c. $\frac{3}{5} > \frac{1}{3}$ **d.** $\frac{5}{8} < \frac{3}{4}$

Write >, <, or = in each ◯.

3.

  $\frac{1}{4}$ ◯ $\frac{3}{4}$

4.

  $\frac{2}{5}$ ◯ $\frac{1}{5}$

5.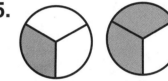

  $\frac{1}{3}$ ◯ $\frac{2}{3}$

6.

  $\frac{1}{3}$ ◯ $\frac{2}{6}$

7.

  $\frac{3}{4}$ ◯ $\frac{5}{8}$

8.

  $\frac{3}{10}$ ◯ $\frac{2}{5}$

....

Solve.

9. Merida painted a picture of a costume parade. She used $\frac{4}{5}$ jar of orange paint and $\frac{3}{5}$ jar of black paint. Which color did she use more of?

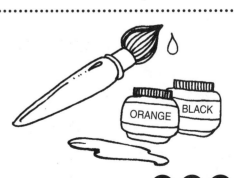

Lay Fraction Tiles on top of each other to check answers.

Name _____ Date _____

Whole Numbers and Mixed Numbers

At the school picnic, Nancy ate a whole sandwich and 1/2 of another sandwich. How many sandwiches did Nancy eat?

Remember

You can make a model to see how many sandwiches Nancy ate.

 $+$

$$1 \quad + \quad \frac{1}{2} \quad = \quad 1\frac{1}{2}$$

whole number + fraction = mixed number

Nancy ate $1\frac{1}{2}$ sandwiches.

Write the whole number or the mixed number to tell how much is shaded.

1.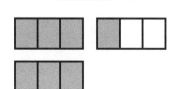

_____

2.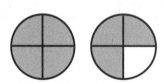

_____

3.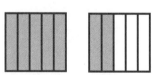

_____

4.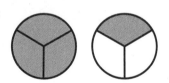

_____

5.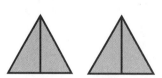

_____

6.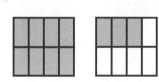

_____

7.

_____

8.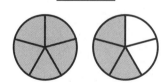

_____

9.

_____

Check answers with Fraction Builder Strips. ◻▶

© Steck-Vaughn Company

Unit 6: Fractions Using Pictorial Models
Geometry 3, SV 5807-8

Name_____ Date _____

Whole Numbers and Mixed Numbers

Write the whole number or the mixed number to show how much is shaded.

1.

2.

3.

_____   _____   _____

4.

5.

6.

_____   _____   _____

7.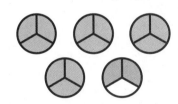

8.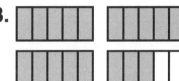

9.

_____   _____   _____

....

Shade the figures to show the mixed numbers.

10. $1\frac{1}{2}$ **11.** $1\frac{3}{4}$ **12.** $2\frac{2}{5}$

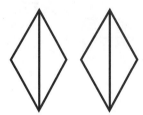   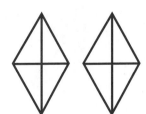   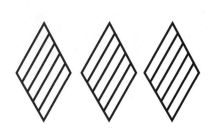

Duplicate fractions with Overhead Fractions.

FRACTIONS USING PICTORIAL MODELS

Whole Numbers and Mixed Numbers

Write the whole number or the mixed number
to show how much is shaded.

1.

2.

3.

_____

4.

5.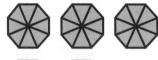

6.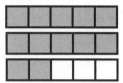

_____

7.

8.

9.

_____

10.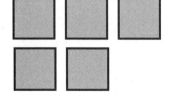

11.

12.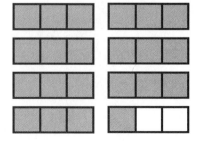

_____

Check answers with Fraction Builder Strips.

Name _____ Date _____

Problem Solving

You can use fractions to show numbers less than a whole. The same fraction can be shown in different ways. For example, all of these shaded parts cover half of the squares.

 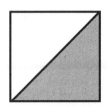 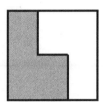 

Solve.

1. How are the shaded parts alike? _____

_____

How are they different? _____

_____

2. How do they compare to the unshaded parts?

_____

3. If each square were a small pizza, would it matter which piece you chose? _____

4. Is it possible to give someone "the bigger half" of a pizza? Tell why or why not. _____

5. Does each picture below show $\frac{1}{4}$? Write *yes* or *no*.

    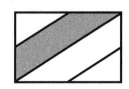

_____ _____ _____ _____ _____

© Steck-Vaughn Company

Problem Solving

Andrew used dot paper to picture fractions.

Write the fraction to show how much he shaded.

1. **2.** **3.** **4.**

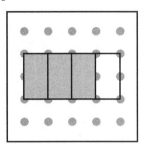   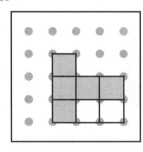   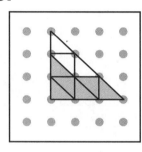   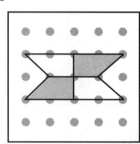

_____   _____   _____   _____

....

Use dot paper to make 6 rectangles of the same size. Make models
of these fractions: $\frac{1}{3}$, $\frac{3}{4}$, $\frac{3}{8}$, $\frac{1}{4}$, $\frac{7}{8}$, and $\frac{1}{2}$. Label each model.
Look at your models.

5. Which is the largest part of a whole? _____

   Which is the smallest part of a whole? _____

6. Compare $\frac{3}{8}$ and $\frac{7}{8}$.

   What do you notice about the denominators? _____

   What do you notice about the numerators? _____

6. Compare $\frac{1}{2}$, $\frac{1}{3}$, and $\frac{1}{4}$.

   What do you notice about the numerators? _____

   Write the fractions in order from the least to the greatest.

   _____

Duplicate figures on Geoboards. ❓▢❯

Name _____ Date _____

Unit 7: Assessment

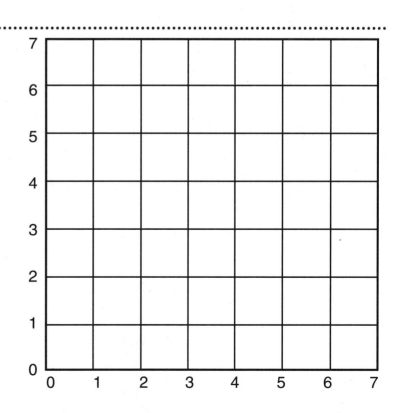

Use the graph to
answer each question.
Which point is at

1. (3,2)? _____   **2.** (4,3)? _____   **3.** (6,2)? _____

Write the number pair for the point.

4. C ____   **5.** D ____   **6.** F ____

....

On the graph, draw a
point for each number pair.

7. V (2,2)

8. W (6,3)

9. X (4,7)

© Steck-Vaughn Company   **87**

Name_____ Date _____

Number Pairs

Number pairs tell you where a point can be found on a graph. Below is a graph that shows stars in a sky. Which star is at (1,4)?

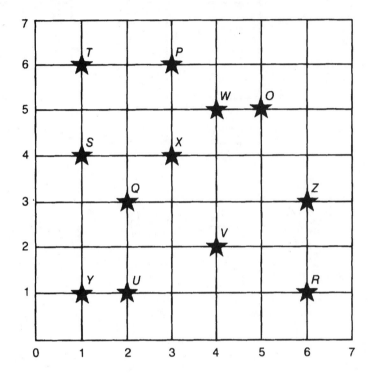

You can find the star by counting. Go to the right to 1 and up to 4.

Star *S* is at (1,4).

....

Use the graph above to answer each question. What star is at

1. (3,4)? _____   **2.** (4,5)? _____   **3.** (1,6)? _____

4. (2,3)? _____   **5.** (6,1)? _____   **6.** (6,3)? _____

7. (5,5)? _____   **8.** (4,2)? _____   **9.** (3,6)? _____

Draw chalk coordinate graph on blacktop. Follow directions to walk to crossing points.

COORDINATE GRAPHS

Number Pairs

Write the number pair for each.

1. the radio tower _____

2. the school _____

3. the library _____

4. the museum _____

5. the theater _____

6. the bank _____

7. the pond _____

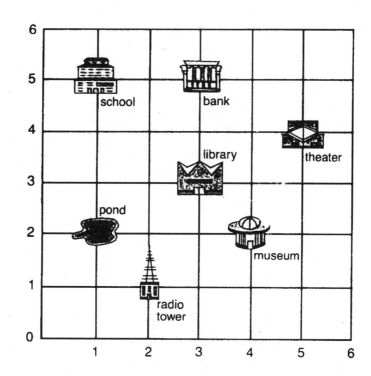

Duplicate coordinate graph on Graph Paper.

Name _____   Date _____

Drawing a Coordinate Graph

Draw points for each number pair on the graph below.

1. (7,4)   **2.** (6,2)   **3.** (2,7)

4. (5,1)   **5.** (4,3)   **6.** (3,6)

7. (4,7)   **8.** (7,7)   **9.** (5,6)

10. (1,2)

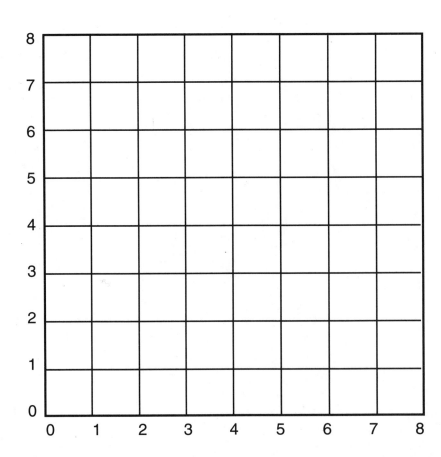

Draw chalk coordinate graph on blacktop. Follow directions to walk to crossing points.

© Steck-Vaughn Company

Unit 7: Coordinate Graphs
Geometry 3, SV 5807-8

COORDINATE GRAPHS

Using a Coordinate Graph

Answer the questions for each graph.

1. What is the number pair for the bicycle? _____

2. Start at 0. Go over 1 and up 5. What do you see? _____

3. What is the number pair for the train? _____

4. What is at the number pair (2,3)? _____

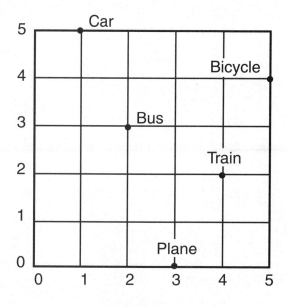

....

Write the letter for each of the following number pairs.

5. (2,5) _____

6. (4,8) _____

7. (5,3) _____

8. What is the number pair for the letter *I*? _____

9. What is the number pair for the letter *D*? _____

10. What is the number pair for the letter *A*? _____

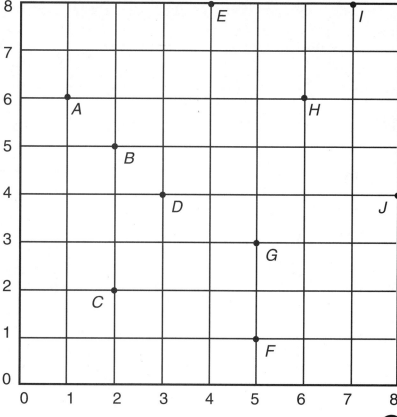

Draw chalk coordinate graph on blacktop. Follow directions to walk to crossing points. ⬛

Name_____ Date _____

Problem Solving

Write the ordered pair for each letter.

1. *A* _____

2. *B* _____

3. *F* _____

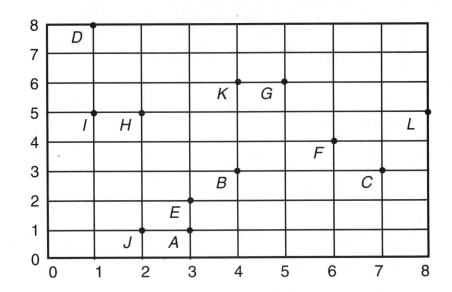

4. Use the grid at the top of the page. If the letter E is moved to the right 2 spaces and up 1 space, what word would you see?

_____

··

Imagine the grid is a map. Tell the location of these places.

5. library _____

6. grocery store _____

7. school _____

8. park _____

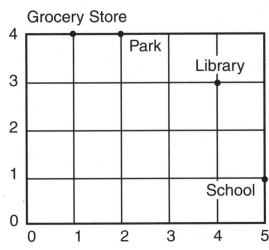

Draw chalk coordinate graph on blacktop. Follow directions to walk to crossing points. ▢

Unit 7: Coordinate Graphs
Geometry 3, SV 5807-8

COORDINATE GRAPHS

Problem Solving

Here's how to use a grid to send messages in code. Each point on the grid stands for a code letter. Use the number pairs to find each letter.

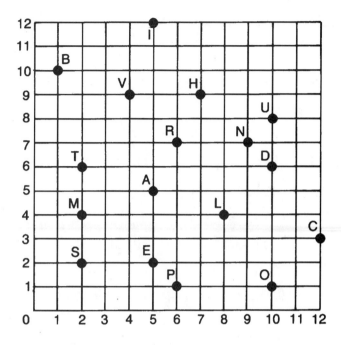

Find the missing code letters in this chart.

→	↑	Letter
2	4	M
5	5	A
2	6	
7	9	

What word was written in code? _____

Use the grid to spell this message.

1.

→	↑	Letter
5	12	

2.

→	↑	Letter
8	4	
10	1	
4	9	
5	2	

3.

→	↑	Letter
2	2	
10	8	
2	4	
2	4	
5	2	
6	7	

4.

→	↑	Letter
4	9	
5	5	
12	3	
5	5	
2	6	
5	12	
10	1	
9	7	

© Steck-Vaughn Company

Unit 7: Coordinate Graphs
Geometry 3, SV 5807-8

COORDINATE GRAPHS

Problem Solving

You can use a grid to make a picture larger or smaller.

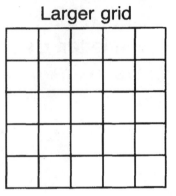

Larger grid

1. Use the larger grid below to make this picture larger.
   - Find a box on the larger grid that matches a box on the small grid with part of the picture in it.
   - Copy that part of the picture on the larger grid.

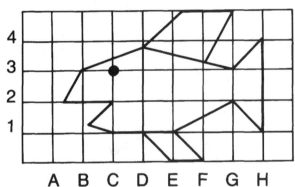

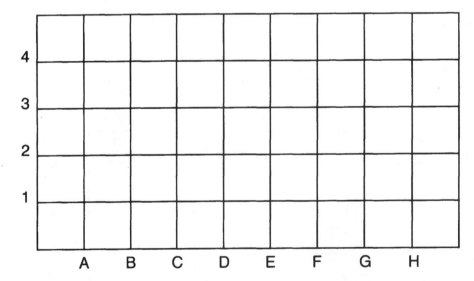

2. Try this with your own picture. Draw a grid on a separate piece of paper. Draw a picture on the grid. Then draw a larger or smaller grid and make your picture larger or smaller.

© Steck-Vaughn Company   **Unit 7: Coordinate Graphs**
Geometry 3, SV 5807-8

Geometry for Primary Grade 3

Unit 1: Basic Ideas of Geometry

Assessment, P. 9
1. $\overline{AB}$, $\overline{BA}$, 2. $\overline{ST}$, $\overline{TS}$, 3. 6, 4. 3, 5. c, e, f, g

P. 10
1. yes, 2. no, 3. no, 4. $\overline{CD}$, $\overline{DC}$, 5. $\overline{QR}$, $\overline{RQ}$, 6. line, 7. line segment, 8. line
9. $\overleftrightarrow{OP}$, $\overleftrightarrow{PO}$, 10. $\overrightarrow{DE}$, $\overrightarrow{ED}$

P. 11
Ring 1 and 3, 4. line segment; $\overline{AB}$, $\overline{BA}$,
5. line; $\overleftrightarrow{XY}$, $\overleftrightarrow{YX}$, 6. line segment; $\overline{ST}$, $\overline{TS}$, 7. b, 8. a, 9. c

P. 12
1. no, 2. yes, 3. no, 4. no, 5. no, 6. yes
7. $\overleftrightarrow{JK}$, $\overleftrightarrow{KJ}$, 8. $\overline{ST}$, $\overline{TS}$, 9. $\overrightarrow{VW}$, $\overrightarrow{WV}$
10. $\overline{ED}$, $\overline{DE}$

P. 13
1. line segment, 2. line, 3. line segment
4. line, 5. line, 6. line segment, 7. $\overrightarrow{FG}$, $\overrightarrow{GF}$,
8. $\overleftrightarrow{XY}$, $\overleftrightarrow{YX}$, 9. $\overrightarrow{ON}$, $\overrightarrow{NO}$, 10. $\overrightarrow{OP}$, $\overrightarrow{PO}$
11. $\overline{ML}$, $\overline{LM}$, 12. $\overleftrightarrow{XW}$, $\overleftrightarrow{WX}$

P. 14
1. yes, 2. no, 3. no, 4. yes, 5. yes, 6. no
7. 3, 8. 6, 9. 5

P. 15
1. yes, 2. no, 3. yes, 4. no, 5. no, 6. yes, 7. 4, 8. 4, 9. 1, 10. 0, 11. 8, 12. 3

P. 16
1. no, 2. yes, 3. no, 4. yes, 5. no, 6. no
7. 4, 8. 5, 9. 3, 10. 5, 11. 5, 12. 4

P. 17
1-2. Student will trace dotted lines.
3-4. Student will trace dotted lines.
Answers will vary on drawings.
5. Shade 0; X 6, 8, 9; Box 2, 3, 5, 7; Ring 1, 4

P. 18
1. Answers will vary., 2. Answers will vary.
3. Color a, b, d, h, Ring c, e, f, g

P. 19
Pieces drawn may vary. Answers to questions should show thought.
1. 3 or 4, 2. yes, 3. 4, 4. 7, 5. 5, 6. 11

P. 20
1. 2.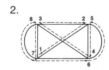

P. 21
Student's drawings do not have to indicate exact perspective, but should show understanding of increase and decrease in size depending on distance.

Unit 2: Plane Figures

Assessment, P. 22
1. triangle, 2. circle, 3. square or rectangle, 4. 3 sides; 3 vertices
5. 4 sides; 4 vertices, 6. 0 sides; 0 vertices, 7. circle, 8. square

P. 23
1. rectangle, 2. circle, 3. triangle, 4. 6 sides; 6 vertices, 5. 4 sides; 4 vertices
6. 4 sides; 4 vertices, 7. 0 sides; 0 vertices

P. 24
1. square and rectangle
2. circle and triangle
3. square, triangle, and rectangle
4. a, 5. b, 6. d, 7. a, c, e, 8. f

P. 25
1. circle, 2. rectangle, 3. triangle
4. square, 5. circle, 6. rectangle
7. rectangle, 8. triangle, 9. square
10. pentagon, 11. circle, 12-14. Answers will vary.

P. 26
1. circle, 2. rectangle, 3. triangle
4. pentagon, 5. circle, 6. square
7. square, 8. rectangle, 9. triangle
10. circle, 11. pentagon, 12. triangle

P. 27
1. All, 2. Some, 3. None, 4. Some, 5. All
6. All

P. 28
Ring 1, 4. Students should draw shape for 2, 3, 5.

P. 29
1. Answers will vary.
2. Answers will vary.
3. yes, 4. no, 5. no, 6. yes, 7. no, 8. yes
9. yes, 10. no, 11. ring first group

P. 30
1-3 Answers will vary, 4. circle, 5. square
6. circle, 7. envelope; rectangle

Unit 3: Solid Figures

Assessment, P. 31
1. 1. 6 faces; 12 edges; 8 vertices, 2. 1 face; 0 edges; 0 vertices, 3. pyramid, 4. rectangular prism, 5. sphere, 6. cylinder

P. 32
1. 6 flat; 0 curved, 2. 1 flat; 1 curved, 3. 6 flat; 0 curved

P. 33
1. 2 flat; 1 curved, 2. 6 flat; 0 curved, 3. 4 faces; 6 edges; 4 vertices, 4. 2 faces; 0 edges; 0 vertices, 5. 6 faces; 12 edges; 8 vertices, 6. 6 faces; 12 edges; 8 vertices, 7. 1 face; 0 edges; 0 vertices
8. 8 faces; 18 edges; 12 vertices

P. 34
1. 1 curved; 0 flat, 2. 1 curved, 2 flat; 3. 1 curved; 1 flat, 4. 6 faces; 12 edges; 8 vertices, 5. 5 faces; 8 edges; 5 vertices
6. 6 faces; 12 edges; 8 vertices, 7. c, 8. a, 9. b

P. 35

Figure	Faces	Edges	Vertices
Cube	6	12	8
Cone	1	0	0
Cylinder	2	0	0
Sphere	0	0	0
Rectangular Prism	6	12	8
Pyramid	5	8	5

P. 36
1. ring book, 2. ring telescope, 3. ring balloon, 4. ring cheese, 5. ring megaphone

P. 37
1. cone, 2. sphere, 3. cube, 4. rectangular prism, 5. cylinder, 6. cylinder, 7. cube
8. rectangular prism

P. 38
1. cylinder, 2. sphere, 3. rectangular prism, 4. pyramid, 5. cube, 6. cone,
7. rectangular prism, 8. pyramid
9. cylinder, 10. Answers will vary.

P. 39
1. pyramid, 2. rectangular prism, 3. cube or rectangular prism, 4. cylinder, 5. sphere

Unit 4: Congruence and Symmetry

Assessment, P. 40
1. no, 2. yes, 3. Ring second figure
4. yes, 5. yes, 6. no

P. 41
1. yes, 2. no, 3. yes, 4. yes, 5. no, 6. no, 7. no, 8. yes, 9. yes

P. 42
1. yes, 2. no, 3. yes, 4. yes, 5. second figure, 6. third figure, 7. third figure
8. Students draw the same-sized figure.

P. 43
1. second figure, 2. third figure, 3. first figure, 4. second figure, 5. second figure, 6. third figure

P. 44
1. no, 2. yes, 3. no, 4. yes, 5. yes, 6. yes

P. 45
1. yes, 2. yes, 3. no, 4. yes, 5. yes, 6. yes, 7. no, 8. yes, 9. yes, 10. no, 11. Answers will vary, but should be lines of symmetry.

P. 46
1. yes, 2. no, 3. no, 4. yes, 5. no, 6. no

P. 47
Ring 1, 2, 4, 6, 8, 9, Draw lines of symmetry in figures 8 and 9. 10. Possible answers: F, G, J, L, N, P, Q, R, S, Z.

P. 48

Geometry for Primary Grade 3

P. 49
1. Answers will vary., 2. Draw horizontal lines through C, D, E, H, I, K, O, X. Draw vertical lines through H, I, M, O, T, U, V, W, X, Y.

Unit 5: Perimeter, Area, and Volume

Assessment, P. 50
1. 12 cm, 2. 5 cm, 3. 12 cm, 4. 12 sq. cm, 5. 7 sq. cm, 6. 6 sq. cm, 7. 12 cubic units, 8. 21 cubic units, 9. 4 cubic units

P. 51
1-7. Answers will vary.

P. 52
1. 12 cm, 2. 12 cm, 3. 10 cm, 4. 10 cm 5. 8 cm, 6. 5 cm, 7. 8 cm, 8. 12 cm, 9. 6 cm

P. 53
1. 6 cm, 2. 8 cm, 3. 10 cm, 4. 16 cm 5. 5 cm, 6. 11 cm

P. 54
1. 6 in., 2. 8 in., 3. 7 in., 4. 6 in., 5. 32 ft 6. 84 in.

P. 55
1. 4 in., 2. 3 in., 3. 148 ft, 4. 70 in.

P. 56
1. 8 in., 2. 6 in., 3. 100 ft, 4. 50 ft, 5. 12 ft 6. 16 ft, 7. 6 ft, 8. 16 ft

P. 57
1. 20 + 15 + 15 = 50
2. 60 - 50 = 10
3. 10, 4. 3 feet, 5. 8 feet, 6. 6 feet 7. 5 feet

P. 58
1-3. Answers will vary., 4. 16 x 4 = 64 steps or 16 + 16 + 16 + 16 = 64 steps

P. 59
1. 6 sq. cm, 2. 6 sq. cm, 3. 7 sq. cm 4. 12 sq. cm, 5. 9 sq. cm, 6. 8 sq. cm

P. 60
1. 8 sq. units, 2. 12 sq. units, 3. 6 sq. units, 4. 16 sq. units, 5. 15 sq. units 6. 18 sq. units, 7-9. Answers will vary. 10. shade 12 sq. units

P. 61
1. 8 sq. cm, 2. 6 sq. cm, 3. 5 sq. cm 4. 3 sq. cm, 5. 6 sq. cm, 6. 6 sq. cm

P. 62
1-3. Answers will vary., 4. 9 sq. units 5. 12 sq. units, 6. 18 sq. units, 7. 8 sq. units, 8. 12 sq. units, 9. 24 sq. units

P. 63
1. 9, 2. 7, 3. 6, 4. 8, 5. A; C, 6. F, 7. 5

P. 64
1. 12 cubic centimeters, 2. 15 cubic centimeters, 3. 27 cubic centimeters 4. 18 cubic centimeters

P. 65
1. 2 cubic units, 2. 4 cubic units 3. 4 cubic units, 4. 8 cubic units 5. 6 cubic units, 6. 3 cubic units 7. 15 cubic units, 8. 18 cubic units 9. 8 cubic units

P. 66
1. 8 cubic units, 2. 12 cubic units 3. 11 cubic units, 4. 7 cubic units 5. 24 cubic units, 6. 15 cubic units 7. 11 cubic units, 8. 3 cubic units 9. 19 cubic units, 10. 24 x 2 = 48 cubic units or 24 + 24 = 48 cubic units

P. 67
1. 8 cubic centimeters, 2. 15 cubic centimeters, 3. 12 cubic centimeters 4. 4 cubic centimeters, 5. 21 cubic centimeters, 6. 20 cubic centimeters 7. 8 cubic centimeters, 8. 18 cubic centimeters, 9. 24 cubic centimeters

P. 68
1. 4 cubic units, 2. 12 cubic units 3. 8 cubic units, 4. 10 cubic units 5. 18 cubic units, 6. 19 cubic units 7. 11 cubic units, 8. 3 cubic units 9. 18 cubic units

Unit 6: Fractions Using Pictorial Models

Assessment, P. 69
1. $\frac{1}{4}$, 2. $\frac{5}{6}$, 3. $\frac{2}{5}$, 4. $\frac{1}{2} = \frac{2}{4}$, 5. $\frac{1}{4} = \frac{2}{8}$ 6. $\frac{3}{6} = \frac{6}{12}$, 7. <, 8. >, 9. <, 10. $2\frac{1}{2}$ 11. $1\frac{3}{4}$, 12. 6

P. 70
1. b, 2. a, 3. d, 4. $\frac{1}{3}$, 5. $\frac{3}{4}$, 6. $\frac{5}{6}$, 7. $\frac{2}{3}$, 8. $\frac{3}{8}$ 9. $\frac{5}{8}$

P. 71
1. $\frac{3}{4}$, 2. $\frac{5}{8}$, 3. $\frac{1}{4}$, 4. $\frac{1}{2}$, 5. $\frac{7}{8}$, 6. $\frac{2}{5}$, 7. $\frac{1}{4}$ 8. $\frac{2}{3}$, 9. $\frac{3}{10}$, 10. $\frac{5}{6}$

P. 72
1. $\frac{4}{5}$, 2. $\frac{2}{4}$, 3. $\frac{1}{3}$, 4. $\frac{3}{5}$, 5. $\frac{5}{6}$, 6. $\frac{2}{6}$, 7. $\frac{4}{5}$ 8. $\frac{4}{4}$, 9. $\frac{1}{3}$, 10. $\frac{2}{5}$, 11. $\frac{4}{6}$, 12. shade one part of sandwich

P. 73
1. a, 2. b, 3. 2, 4. 6, 5. 2

P. 74
1. $\frac{6}{10}$, 2. $\frac{2}{4}$, 3. $\frac{4}{10}$, 4. $\frac{2}{3} = \frac{4}{6}$, 5. $\frac{1}{2} = \frac{5}{10}$ 6. $\frac{4}{5} = \frac{8}{10}$, 7. $\frac{3}{4} = \frac{6}{8}$, 8. $\frac{1}{2} = \frac{3}{6}$, 9. $\frac{3}{6} = \frac{5}{10}$

P. 75
1. 2, 2. 4, 3. 12, 4. 4, 5. 8, 6. 3

P. 76
1. c, 2. b, 3. a, 4. b, 5. a, 6. c, 7. $\frac{4}{8}$ & $\frac{1}{2}$ 8. $\frac{1}{4}$ & $\frac{2}{8}$, 9. $\frac{4}{5}$ & $\frac{8}{10}$, 10-12. Students will correctly shade fractions.

P. 77
1. true, 2. false, 3. true, 4. false, 5. true 6. false, 7. 4, 8. 1, 9. 4, 10. 2, 11. 1 12. 3, 13. 2, shade 2 parts

P. 78
1. <, 2. <, 3. =, 4. <, 5. >, 6. <

P. 79
1. 2/3, 2. 3/4, 3. 3/7, 4. 5/8, 5. <, 6. > 7. >, 8. <, 9. =, 10. <

P. 80
1. <, 2. >, 3. >, 4. <, 5. =, 6. >, 7. =, 8. > 9. <, 10. more milk

P. 81
1. b, 2. d, 3. <, 4. >, 5. <, 6. =, 7. >, 8. < 9. She used more orange paint.

P. 82
1. $1\frac{1}{3}$, 2. $1\frac{3}{4}$, 3. $1\frac{2}{5}$, 4. $2\frac{1}{3}$, 5. 2, 6. $1\frac{3}{8}$ 7. $1\frac{1}{4}$, 8. $1\frac{3}{5}$, 9. $1\frac{1}{2}$

P. 83
1. $1\frac{3}{4}$, 2. $2\frac{1}{2}$, 3. $3\frac{3}{8}$, 4. 2, 5. $2\frac{6}{10}$, 6. $1\frac{5}{8}$ 7. $4\frac{2}{3}$, 8. $3\frac{3}{8}$, 9. 4, 10-12. Students will correctly shade figures.

P. 84
1. $1\frac{1}{4}$, 2. 3, 3. $2\frac{2}{5}$, 4. $3\frac{3}{10}$, 5. $4\frac{5}{8}$, 6. $4\frac{1}{2}$ 7. 5, 8. $5\frac{5}{6}$, 9. 6, 10. $5\frac{5}{10}$, 11. $7\frac{3}{4}$, 12. $7\frac{1}{3}$

P. 85
1. all show $\frac{1}{2}$; different shape,
2. They each show $\frac{1}{2}$ of the drawing; 3. no 4. No, halves are equal in size, 5. yes, no, no, yes, no

P. 86
1. $\frac{3}{4}$, 2. $\frac{5}{7}$, 3. $\frac{6}{9}$, 4. $\frac{4}{4}$, 5. $\frac{7}{8}$, $\frac{1}{4}$, 6. The denominators are the same; The numerators are different, 7. The numerators are all 1; $\frac{1}{4}$, $\frac{1}{3}$, $\frac{1}{2}$

Unit 7: Coordinate Graphs

Assessment, P. 87
1. *I*, 2. *G*, 3. *J*, 4. (4,5), 5. (6,5), 6. (5,4) 7-9.

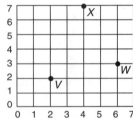

P. 88
1. *X*, 2. *W*, 3. *T*, 4. *Q*, 5. *R*, 6. *Z*, 7. *O*, 8. *V*, 9. *P*

P. 89
1. (2,1), 2. (1,5), 3. (3,3), 4. (4,2), 5. (5,4), 6. (3,5), 7. (1,2)

P. 90

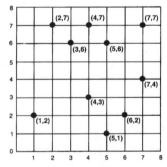

P. 91
1. (5,4), 2. car, 3. (4,2), 4. bus, 5. *B*, 6. *E*, 7. *G*, 8. (7,8), 9. (3,4), 10. (1,6)

P. 92
1. (3,1), 2. (4,3), 3. (6,4), 4. BE, 5. (4,3), 6. (1,4), 7. (5,1), 8. (2,4)

P. 93
What word was written in code? math
1. *I*, 2. LOVE, 3. SUMMER, 4. VACATION

P. 94
Student will draw fish on grid.

© Steck-Vaughn Company

Answer Key
Geometry 3, SV 5807-8